Poetry of the 1940s

KU-133-257

*An anthology
selected and edited by*

Howard Sergeant

Longman

LONGMAN GROUP LIMITED
London
*Associated companies, branches and
representatives throughout the world*

Introduction and Notes © Longman Group Ltd 1970
All rights reserved. No part of this publication may be
reproduced, stored in a retrieval system, or transmitted
in any form or by any means, electronic, mechanical,
photocopying, recording, or otherwise, without the prior
permission of the Copyright owner.
First published 1970

SBN 582 34168 X

THE EDITOR

Howard Sergeant is the founder and editor of the poetry magazine, *Outposts*. He
has published two volumes of poetry and three volumes of literary criticism, and
edited many anthologies of poetry, including *Commonwealth Poems of Today* (Murray,
1907), *New Voices of the Commonwealth* (Evans, 1968), *Poems from Hospital* (Allen &
Unwin, 1968), *Poetry from Africa* (Pergamon, 1968), *Poetry from Australia* (Pergamon,
1969), and *The Swinging Rainbow*, for children (Evans, 1969). He is British Common-
wealth Editor on the editorial board of Borestone Mountain Poetry Awards, reader
and adviser for the Gregory Awards, and a member of the Board of Management
of Universities' Poetry.

Poetry of the 1940s

PORTREE HIGH SCHOOL
753
INVERNESS-SHIRE

LONGMAN ENGLISH SERIES

This series includes both period anthologies and selections from the work of individual authors. The introductions and notes have been based upon the most up-to-date criticism and scholarship and the editors have been chosen for their special knowledge of the material.

General Editor Maurice Hussey

*Available in paperback

Contents

PART TWO—POETS OF THE AFTERMATH

Acknowledgements

We are grateful to the following for permission to reproduce copyright material:

George Allen & Unwin for 'Raider's Dawn', 'All Day it has rained', 'The Public Gardens', 'To Edward Thomas', 'Postscript: For Gweno' from *Raiders' Dawn* by Alun Lewis and for 'Infantry', 'Song', 'Goodbye', 'Karanje Village', 'The Mahratta Ghats', 'Water Music', 'The Peasants' from *Ha! Ha! Among The Trumpets* by Alun Lewis; Jonathan Cape Limited for 'The Door and the Window', 'Lives', 'Lessons of the War: I Naming of Parts', 'II Judging Distances', 'III Unarmed Combat', 'The Desert: III South' and 'Tintagel: IV Iseult La Belle' from *A Map of Verona* and *The Novel Since 1939* by Henry Reed; J. M. Dent & Sons Limited for 'The Conversation of Prayer', 'A refusal to Mourn the Death, By Fire, of a Child in London', 'Poem in October', 'This Side of Truth', 'To Others Than You', 'The Hunchback in the Park', 'A Winter's Tale', 'In My Craft or Sullen Art' and 'Fern Hill' from *Death and Entrances* by Dylan Thomas; Andre Deutsch Limited for 'Soliloquy in an Air Raid', 'Epitaph on a Bombing Victim', 'The Middle of War', 'Y.M.C.A. Writing Room', 'Harbour Ferry' from *Middle of a War*, 'In Africa', 'Askari's Song', 'The Green Hills of Africa', 'The Giraffes', 'The Plains', 'What is Terrible', 'During a Bombardment by V-Weapons' from *A Lost Season*, both by Roy Fuller; Faber & Faber Limited for 'The Wayside Station', 'The Narrow Place', 'The Good Man in Hell', 'The Castle', 'Moses', 'The Labyrinth', 'The Child Dying', 'The Combat', 'The Interrogation', 'The Good Town', 'Soliloquy', 'The Transfiguration' from *Collected Poems 1921–1958* by Edwin Muir, for 'The Collier' from *The Ballad of the Mari Lwyd* and 'Sardine Fishers at Daybreak', 'The Feather', 'The Healing of the Leper', 'Lace-maker' from *The Lady With the Unicorn* both by Vernon Watkins, for 'Rockferns', 'Waiting for Spring 1943', 'The Evacuees' from *Five Rivers* by Norman Nicholson and 'Naaman', 'To a Child before Birth', 'Across the Estuary', 'Silecroft Shore' from *Rock Face* by Norman Nicholson, for 'Time Eating', 'The Marvel', 'Simplify me when I'm Dead', 'Egyptian Sentry, Corniche, Alexandria', 'Behaviour of Fish in an Egyptian Tea Garden', 'Cairo Jag', 'Vergissmeinicht', 'I listen to the Desert Wind', 'How to Kill', 'Enfidaville', 'Aristocrats', 'On a Return from Egypt' from *Collected Poems* by Keith Douglas; author, author's agents and Macmillan & Company Limited for 'Still Falls the Rain', 'Lullaby', 'Serenade: Any Man to Any Woman' from *Street Songs*, 'A Mother to her Dead Child' and 'Heart and Mind' from *Green Song* and 'Dirge for the New Sunrise', 'The Shadow of Cain', 'The Canticle of the Rose' from *The Canticle of the Rose* all by Dame Edith Sitwell; Routledge & Kegan Paul Limited for 'Advice for a Journey', 'The Wilderness', 'The Expected Guest' from *The Cruel Solstice*, 'Europe's Prisoners' from *Collected Poems* and 'Troll Kings' from *The Iron Laurel* all by Sidney Keyes.

Foreword

It should be emphasised that this anthology is not offered as a collection of the best poems produced during the 1940s; nor is its purpose to present examples of the work of all the poets who happened to be writing during that turbulent period. On the contrary, it provides substantial selections from the work of poets considered to be the most *characteristic* of the decade, though it is hoped that, as a result of this editorial policy, it will include many of the best poems and represent some of the most outstanding poets of the time. Admittedly, the prominent figures of the 'thirties—Auden, Spender, Day Lewis, and MacNeice—were still very much in evidence, but because the poetic climate had changed their poems no longer reflected the prevailing attitudes, moods and ideas. It is also true that T. S. Eliot's *Four Quartets*, one of the most important volumes of the whole period, was published in 1944, but though Eliot exercised a tremendous influence upon other poets of the time (notably Sidney Keyes, Norman Nicholson, Anne Ridler and Edith Sitwell), he remained a dominant figure standing somewhat aloof from the general scene. Similarly, Robert Graves continued to pursue his own line of development outside the main trends of the forties, to make a much greater impact upon the next generation of poets in the following decade. John Betjeman, Ronald Bottrall, Roy Campbell, Walter de la Mare, Laurie Lee, William Plomer, and other admirable poets have also been excluded from consideration here because their work falls outside the scope of this collection.

Since neither poets nor poetic trends are influenced by chronological lines of division, it may seem an artificial arrangement, if convenient for literary critics and historians, to consider British poetry decade by decade; yet there is every justification for considering the forties as a distinct and separate period. The outbreak of war set a clear demarcation line between the poetry produced before and after September 1939; so much so that the difference can be discerned in the work of individual poets. Roy Fuller, for instance, has remarked upon the new 'briskness and precision' to be seen in a poem of his own, written only two months after war had been declared. There can be no doubt that, so far as poetry was concerned, there was a distinct change in ideas, outlook, response to the general situation, and in forms of expression. As Alan Ross observed in his survey of *Poetry 1945–50* for the British Council: 'The war more or less sealed off the main characteristics of the poetry of the thirties. The totality of its nature, its provision of an external common experience, produced ready-made themes which a serious poet could hardly avoid.' If the outbreak of war decisively ended the thirties, with its socially conscious poetry, the cessation of hostilities— or rather, the dropping of the atom bomb in 1945—proved an even more conclusive line of demarcation. The nuclear age had begun in earnest and things could never be quite the same again. As the forties can, then, be divided into two distinct periods, it seems appropriate to consider the poets of the time under two headings—'Poets of Wartime' and 'Poets of the Aftermath'. It should be stressed, however, that this is not to suggest, or even imply, that the selected poets of either period can be regarded as a group in any way.

Probably more nonsense has been written about the poetry of the 1940s than that of any other period in literary history. So much is this the case that before the period can be seen in anything like its right perspective and discussed in meaningful terms, it becomes necessary to expose the biased and inaccurate version of the forties put forward by the predominant group of poets in the following decade, known collectively as The Movement and comprising such poets as Philip Larkin, D. J. Enright, Donald Davie and their imitators; a version which, owing to successful publicity and the reluctance to examine their comments objectively, has been responsible for the neglect of some very talented poets. New poets often form groups of one kind or another as a means of securing an audience, and in order to establish their claims to a hearing, or to emphasise certain aspects of poetry which they feel may have been overlooked, they invariably call attention to themselves by denouncing the ideas or styles of the preceding generation of poets. In a way it is all part of an established procedure for catching the limelight, and during the last fifty years English poetry has been extraordinarily susceptible to such literary manoeuvres. As G. S. Fraser observes in his *The Modern Writer and his World*, 'the reputation of a decade is often an agreed fiction. It is part of literary tactics for every new generation of young men to run down their immediate predecessors'. Usually no one takes it very seriously and little harm is done. Within a few years such groups disperse, having made their points (and possibly a few reputations) in the process, and the genuine poets amongst them pursue their own lines of development. True to type, the Movement in its turn lost its original impetus and has disintegrated, yet its highly coloured version of the forties remains to be assessed for what it is really worth.

According to the myth so assiduously built up, it would appear that after the sociopolitical group of the thirties had disappeared as a result of the war, the surrealists and a group of poets calling themselves the New Apocalypse were almost the only poets writing throughout the forties, and that not until the Movement made the headlines in 1954 was poetry finally delivered from their all-pervasive and unhealthy influence. One appreciates, of course, that to establish their own claims the Movement poets felt obliged to set up aunt sallies in order to knock them down again, but one can justifiably complain that, if a representative forties group had to be selected for the purpose, a much more appropriate group than the New Apocalypse might have been chosen. There was, after all, plenty of choice—with the war poets, personalists, anarchists, existentialists, new romantics, the Cairo group, and the religious group influenced by Eliot, to say nothing of the various regionalist and nationalist movements, all clamouring for attention throughout the period in question. Since there was so much diversity in style and outlook, so many conflicting ideas about the nature of poetry, so much experiment and so many individualist poets striking out on lines of their own, perhaps the only thing that can be said with any certainty is that no single group could be regarded as representative of the forties—the Apocalyptics least of all.

There is, in fact, good reason for treating the Apocalyptic school of poets as a hangover from the thirties. To use the words of its founder, Henry Treece (*Outposts, No. 12*), 'the unfortunately-named Apocalyptic movement was founded—if so distinguished a verb may be applied to a midnight meeting of young men in a Leeds garret', by J. F. Hendry, Dorian Cooke, Nicholas Moore and Treece himself in 1938. It was mainly a reaction to the mechanistic thinking and sociopolitical trends of the thirties, and the first collection of their work, *The New Apocalypse*, was published in 1939. It is true that a second collection, *The White Horseman*, appeared in 1941, but by 1943 the movement, if it can so be described, was over; one might almost say 'exhausted'. To quote Henry Treece again, 'by the time the third anthology appeared there seemed little point in proceeding further. The movement had come into being largely to vindicate the Romantic outlook . . . and by 1943 they felt this object had been largely accomplished.' No doubt they contributed something to the poetic climate and made an impact upon some of the younger writers of the time, but to credit the Apocalyptics with more influence than that is to lose one's sense of perspective.

There is an even stronger case for associating Surrealism with the previous decade, since it was introduced to this country by Herbert Read and David Gascoigne in the mid-thirties; and its leading exponents, Dylan Thomas and George Barker, both published their first books about the same time (*Eighteen Poems* by Dylan Thomas, 1934; *Poems* by George Barker, 1935). Yet we find A. Alvarez making such questionable statements as : 'So when the war finally broke out, poetry lurched into a kind of nervous breakdown. . . . What was missing from the poetry of the 1940s was simply a voice, distinct, alive and humanly reasonably speaking. Everyone was shouting' (*International Literary Annual*, edited by John Wain). One of the aims of *Poetry of the 1940s* is to present a more reliable account of the period and to demonstrate that there were voices worth hearing.

As one might expect in wartime, a lot of bad verse was produced; but what period has been free from bad verse? If the period is to be seen objectively and constructively, its best work ought to be properly evaluated. Quite apart from the wartime poets, Keith Douglas, Alun Lewis, Sidney Keyes, Roy Fuller and Henry Reed, those who emerged during the forties include John Heath-Stubbs, Laurence Durrell, Laurie Lee, Anne Ridler, Norman Nicholson, Kathleen Raine, Vernon Watkins, Alan Ross,

R. S. Thomas, F. T. Prince, Norman MacCaig, Charles Causley, Terence Tiller and David Wright, to mention a few at random. Several of the older poets developed their styles significantly (Edwin Muir, Edith Sitwell, Roy Campbell, Louis MacNeice, Herbert Read, Robert Graves, and Patrick Kavanagh); and amongst the books published were such notable volumes as *Deaths and Entrances* by Dylan Thomas, *The Song of the Cold* by Edith Sitwell, *The Labyrinth* by Edwin Muir, and what can only be regarded as one of the finest long poems of the century, Eliot's *Four Quartets.*

PART ONE

Poets of Wartime

INTRODUCTION

It is, by this time, generally acknowledged that the war years, 1939–45, produced an extraordinary interest in poetry, not only amongst the casual readers of poetry magazines and anthologies, but throughout the reading public. Despite the restrictions of wartime, a considerable number of young men and women discovered in poetry a vital form of expression (most people over school-leaving age were in the Forces or some branch of national service). Poems were written under all sorts of conditions— in crowded billets, bars, factory and Naafi canteens, and isolated nissen huts; on active service or in between working shifts. It would be absurd to suggest that these young writers were responsible for any work which could be described as of major importance; under the conditions in which they were compelled to write, it would have been astonishing if they had. But there can be no doubt that some of them, Keith Douglas, Alun Lewis, Sidney Keyes, Henry Reed, Roy Fuller, Alan Ross, Charles Causley and several others, managed to produce work of a remarkably high standard.

To some extent this revival of interest in poetry was inevitable. With the loss of personal freedom and the restrictions imposed upon the individual by the necessities of modern warfare, people are driven back upon their emotions and it is natural that they should seek an outlet, if not a reality, in the arts most accessible to them, music and poetry. In the presence of suffering and death on a vast scale, they become more aware of themselves, their loneliness and nostalgia, their unvoiced fears and aspirations, and they experience a powerful urge to make themselves articulate. Much of the work produced during the war years was immature and unpolished, but at least it was genuine and free from literary pretentiousness. If these young poets were concerned with fundamentals, they were certainly not afraid to take their material from sources available to the layman, and to attempt by whatever powers of intuition and observation they possessed to wring some meaning out of life.

The poets of the following decade prided themselves upon their 'restraint', for being 'anti-phoney, anti-wet'. Anyone studying the work of the forties properly will be able to find just as many 'anti-phoney, anti-wet' poems as were ever produced in the fifties, and a restraint that was quite remarkable in the situations in which it was exhibited. Poems which clearly anticipate the trends of both the fifties and the sixties can also be found. It was, then, an exciting and experimental period, with a wide variety of styles in evidence. There was little in the way of enthusiasm or heroics. In one of his letters, Keith Douglas expressed the views of his generation when he said: 'To be sentimental or emotional now is dangerous to oneself and to others. To trust anyone or to admit any hope of a better world is criminally foolish, as foolish as it is to stop working for it. It sounds silly to say work without hope, but it can be done; it's only a form of insurance; it doesn't mean work hopelessly.' Even the most romantically inclined of these wartime poets, Sidney Keyes, had no illusions in this respect:

> Go forth, my friends, the raven is no sibyl;
> Break the clouds' anger with your unchanged faces.
> You'll find, maybe, the dream under the hill—
> But never Canaan, nor any golden mountain.*

It is true that nothing can be matched with the pity, indignation and bitterness of Wilfred Owen, or the violent satire of Siegfried Sassoon, of the first world war, though Keith Douglas's 'Vergissmeinicht' and 'Aristocrats' do seem to have some affinity with Owen's work and Henry Reed's 'Lessons of the War' are as penetrating as, and a good deal more subtle than, Sassoon's outbursts; but it should be remembered that Owen and Sassoon were meeting the horrors of modern war for the first time. There was, in fact, little of the trench warfare which so appalled these poets— the second world war was characterised by tank manoeuvres and swift movement of armies on land, submarine activities and convoys at sea, and heavy bombing of cities from the air. Moreover, the poets of the second world war were in a completely different position. The Japanese invasion of China, Italy's attack upon Abyssinia, the Spanish Civil War, and finally the Munich

*'Advice for a Journey'.

2

agreement which allowed Hitler to seize Czechoslovakia, had all made impacts upon the younger generation. For years their minds had been prepared for all the terrors associated with war fought under modern conditions; so much so that they regarded the first few months of inactive warfare as 'phoney'. The actual fighting, when it did come, could add nothing to the hopelessness and disillusionment to which they had been conditioned by the events of the 1930s. War, they had come to believe, was inevitable sooner or later.

The prevalent moods were those of personal loss and loneliness, frustration, compassion for all caught up like themselves in the turmoils of war, and the need to preserve whatever might be felt of value. As Henry Reed expressed it:

> Things may be the same again; and we must fight
> Not in the hope of winning but rather of keeping
> Something alive . . .

Much has been said about their obsession with 'the single poetic theme of Life and Death', but it might be said that by their very acceptance of death, the emphasis was thrown upon life and the interpretation of those values necessary to the fulfilment of the individual. About the time of Dunkirk, Alan Rook (staff captain, R.A.) wrote:

> What hope for the future? Can we who see the tide
> ebbing along the shore, the greedy, lined
> with shadows, dare with puny words support
> a future which belongs to others? Dare we bind
>
> now, at this last moment of sunshine above
> the crests of oncoming events, like waves which move
> remorselessly nearer, future generations
> with sacrifice? We who taught hate, expect them to love?*

F. T. Prince's 'Soldiers Bathing', one of the best poems of the war, reflects the officer's compassionate feeling for the men under his command (Prince was a captain in the Intelligence Corps., M.E.F.):

* Dunkirk Pier

All's pathos now. The body that was gross,
Rank, ravening, disgusting in the act or in repose,
All fever, filth and sweat, its bestial strength
And bestial decay, by pain and labour grows at length
Fragile and luminous. Poor bare forked animal,
Conscious of his desires and needs and
          flesh that rise and fall,
Stands in the soft air, tasting after toil
The sweetness of his nakedness; letting the sea-waves
          coil
Their frothy tongues about his feet, forgets
His hatred of war, its terrible pressure that begets
That machinery of death and slavery,
Each being a slave and making slaves of others . . .

ALUN LEWIS was one of the most outstanding poets of the war years but his reputation as a poet has been obscured by the tendency of critics to 'write off' the forties as a period when 'poetry lurched into a kind of nervous breakdown', though the phrase has no relevance at all when applied to Lewis's poetry. Although his first book, *Raiders' Dawn*, was not published until 1942, it is interesting to note that over a third of its contents had been written before the outbreak of war in 1939, and the influence of other poets can be traced in the earlier work. Since he was born at Cwmaman, near Aberdare, it was natural that he should be conscious of his Welsh heritage and that he should be concerned with the Welsh landscape and people, as an early poem, 'The Mountain over Aberdare', shows:

> From this high quarried ledge I see
> The place for which the Quakers once
> Collected clothes, my father's home,
> Our stubborn bankrupt village sprawled
> In jaded dusk beneath its nameless hills;
> The drab streets strung across the cwm,
> Derelict workings, tips of slag
> The gospellers and gamblers use
> And children scrutting for coal
> That winter dole cannot purvey;

> Allotments where the collier digs
> While engines hack the coal within his brain . . .

yet he was never a vociferous nationalist. His experiences in wartime, combined with his inner sense of conflict, seemed to have had the effect of crystallising his ideas and focusing them upon the human condition, though the universal element in his poetry was never more clearly expressed than in what might be described as his personal lyrics, such as 'Postscript: for Gweno' and 'Goodbye' (written on his departure for India):

> We made the universe to be our home,
> Our nostrils took the wind to be our breath,
> Our hearts are massive towers of delight,
> We stride across the seven seas of death.
>
> Yet when all's done you'll keep the emerald
> I placed upon your finger in the street;
> And I will keep the patches that you sewed
> On my old battledress tonight, my sweet.

As he wrote in one of his letters, '. . . there doesn't seem to be any question more directly relevant than this one, of what survives of all the beloved, I find myself quite unable to express at once the passion of Love, the coldness of Death (Death *is* cold), and the fire that beats against resignation, "acceptance". Acceptance seems so spiritless, protest so vain. In between the two I live.'

His second collection of poems, *Ha! Ha! Among the Trumpets*, published posthumously, shows a marked improvement, though Lewis was still striving for a personal philosophy as well as for the individual command of language in which to express it. In October 1942 he left England for service in India, and most of his second volume is concerned with his reactions to conditions in India and Burma. The book is divided into three sections— 'England', 'The Voyage', and 'India'—and if it contains some dramatic appraisals of his wartime experience (such as 'Observation Post', 'The Raid', 'Burma Casualty', 'In Hospital: Poona', and 'Assault Convoy', etc.), it is in Lewis's vision of humanity within the changing, and yet unchanging, pattern of history, that his maturity is most clearly revealed:

> Across scorched hills and trampled crops
> The soldiers struggle by.
> History staggers in their wake.
> The peasants watch them die.

KEITH DOUGLAS, like Lewis, was killed on active service, but seems to have been more prepared for military service and life as a British officer—indeed, in some respects he seems almost to have welcomed the opportunity of testing himself in battle—and had little time to become introspective or develop a concern for society in general. As Ted Hughes has remarked, 'war was his ideal subject; the burning away of all human pretensions in the ray cast by death'. He was, in fact, an excellent soldier, and his poetry conveys something of the excitement of his experience as a tough young tank officer, fascinated by what he observed, looking death straight in the eye, so to speak; though never allowing his feelings to overcome the tight-lipped restraint typical of the product of the English public school:

> Remember me when I'm dead
> and simplify me when I'm dead.

> As the processes of earth
> strip off the colour and the skin;
> take the brown hair and blue eye

> and leave me simpler than at birth,
> when hairless I came howling in
> as the moon entered the cold sky.

SIDNEY KEYES, who was killed in the Tunisian campaign in April 1943, just before his twenty-first birthday, has been described as 'the spokesman of his generation'. To judge by the intensity of his work, it might seem that he had a premonition of his early death. Keyes conceived the poet's function to be that of expressing 'the eternal meaning which resides in the physical world, and show the relationship between the eternal and its physical counterpart'. With his acute sense of guilt and individual responsibility for the human predicament, Keyes sought the 'eternal meaning' through his philosophy of renunciation, fittingly expressed in the long poem, 'The Wilderness':

> There is no parting
> From friends, but only from the ways of friendship;
> Nor from our lovers, though the forms of love
> Change often as the landscape of this journey
> To the dark valley where the gold bird burns.
> I say, Love is a wilderness and these bones
> Proclaim no failure, but the death of youth.
> We say, You must be ready for the desert
> Even among the orchards starred with blossom,
> Even in spring, or at the waking moment
> When the man turns to the woman, and both are afraid.
> All who would save their life must find the desert—
> The lover, the poet, the girl who dreams of Christ,
> And the swift runner, crowned with another laurel:
> They all must face the sun, the red rock desert,
> And see the burning of the metal bird . . .

It is unfortunate that HENRY REED has written so little poetry, for he undoubtedly possesses genuine talent, and the pieces which make up his 'Lessons of the War' ('Naming of Parts', 'Judging Distances' and 'Unarmed Combat') are, despite the mocking approach—perhaps because of it—amongst the most outstanding, as well as the most amusing, poems of the wartime period. It is not insignificant, however, that Reed deals with the training procedures of the Army rather than the actual conditions of warfare, which may explain why he is able to distance his subject so well. The sequence might be more aptly entitled 'Lessons of Training for War'. Nevertheless, in his witty and intelligent approach, he does express the individual's sense of frustration and bitterness at the violent interruption of his personal life in such lines as:

> There may be dead ground in between:
>> and I may not have got
> The knack of judging a distance; I will only venture
> A guess that perhaps between me and the apparent
>> lovers
> (Who, incidentally, appear by now to have finished)
> At seven o clock from the houses,
>> is roughly a distance
>> Of about one year and a half.

Curiously enough, the very success of these pieces as 'war poems' may have contributed to his neglect as a poet. For though most of the poems in his volume, *A Map of Verona* (1946), were written in wartime, these three well-known poems are the only ones directly concerned with the war. The contemplative poems, 'The Desert', and 'Tintagel' sequences, the dramatic monologues ('Chrysothemis' and 'Philoctetes'), and some of his lyrics, are equally deserving of attention.

Although ROY FULLER started writing in the thirties and had his first volume, *Poems*, published in 1939, it was not until the period of wartime, which both widened and intensified his experience, that he began to develop the characteristic style which has made him one of the most outstanding poets of the postwar years. Since he was deeply concerned above all with man in relation to his environment and society—that is, with man as a social and political animal—it is hardly surprising that he should be influenced by Auden and the 'social' poets of the thirties in the initial stages. This is not to imply that his work was derivative in the usual sense: still less to suggest that he appropriated the political ideas of the thirties simply because they were fashionable at the time, as so many other poets appear to have done; for Fuller has remained consistent in his thinking and attitudes throughout his poetic career, whereas even the most vociferous exponents of the social conscience seemed to abandon their positions with the outbreak of hostilities. Yet the effort to accommodate the didactic style of the thirties, to say nothing of the Audenesque mannerisms, within his own Marxist conception of the human condition, resulted in clumsiness and a straining after effect.

Almost with the outbreak of war, Fuller found his voice, as if he had needed such a stimulus to develop and activate his style. In his second book, *The Middle of a War*, he writes with a new irony and precision about the effects of war upon himself:

> My photograph already looks historic.
> The promising youthful face, the matelot's collar,
> Say: 'This one is remembered for a lyric.
> His place and period—nothing could be duller.'

Its position is already indicated—
The son or brother in the album; pained
The expression and the garments dated,
His fate so obviously preordained.

upon his friends:

Today my friends were drafted; they are about
To be exploded, to be scattered over
That coloured square which in reality
Is a series of scenes, is boredom, cover,

Nostalgia, labour, death.

and upon the ordinary man:

Reader, could his limbs be found
Here would lie a common man:
History inflicts no wound
But explodes what it began,
And with its enormous lust
For division splits the dust.
Do not ask his nation; that
Was History's confederate.

As a naval rating in the Fleet Air Arm, Roy Fuller was stationed
in Africa for a time and in such poems as 'In Africa', 'The Green
Hills of Africa', 'The Giraffes', 'The Plains', 'Askari's Song',
and 'The Tribes', (all from *A Lost Season*, 1944), we can see a new
vitality at work, which, combined with descriptive powers of
exceptional sharpness and a rare capacity for social analysis,
added a new dimension to Fuller's poetry, seen perhaps at its
best in 'What is Terrible':

The year, the month, the day, the minute, at war
Is terrible and my participation
And that of all the world is terrible.
My living now must bear the laceration
Of the herd, and always will. What's done

To me is done to many. I can see
No ghosts, but only the fearful actual
Lives of my comrades. If the empty whitish
Horror is ever to be flushed and real,
It must be for them and changed by them all.

Alun Lewis

from RAIDERS' DAWN 1942

Raiders' Dawn

Softly the civilised
Centuries fall,
Paper on paper,
Peter on Paul.

And lovers waking
From the night—
Eternity's masters,
Slaves of Time—
Recognise only
The drifting white
Fall of small faces
In pits of lime.

Blue necklace left
On a charred chair
Tells that Beauty
Was startled there.

All Day it has Rained

All day it has rained, and we on the edge of the moors
Have sprawled in our bell-tents, moody and dull as boors,
Groundsheets and blankets spread on the muddy ground
And from the first grey wakening we have found

No refuge from the skirmishing fine rain
And the wind that made the canvas heave and flap
And the taut wet guy-ropes ravel out and snap.
All day the rain has glided, wave and mist and dream,
Drenching the gorse and heather, a gossamer stream
Too light to stir the acorns that suddenly
10 Snatched from their cups by the wild south-westerly
Pattered against the tent and our upturned dreaming faces.
And we stretched out, unbuttoning our braces,
Smoking a woodbine, darning dirty socks,
Reading the Sunday papers—I saw a fox
And mentioned it in the note I scribbled home;—
And we talked of girls, and dropping bombs on Rome,
And thought of the quiet dead and the loud celebrities
Exhorting us to slaughter, and the herded refugees;
—Yet thought softly, morosely of them, and as indifferently
20 As of ourselves or those whom we
For years have loved, and will again
Tomorrow maybe love; but now it is the rain
Possesses us entirely, the twilight and the rain.

And I can remember nothing dearer or more to my heart
Than the children I watched in the woods on Saturday
Shaking down the burning chestnuts for the schoolyard's merry
     play,
Or the shaggy patient dog who followed me
By Sheet and Steep and up the wooded scree
To the Shoulder o' Mutton where Edward Thomas
     brooded long
30 On death and beauty—till a bullet stopped his song.

The Public Gardens

Only a few top-heavy holly-hocks, wilting in arid beds.
Frayed lawns,
Twin sycamores storing the darkness massively under
     balconies of leaf,

And an empty rococo bandstand—strangely unpopular
Saturday evening in the public gardens.

But wait: These take their places:—

A thin little woman in black stockings and a straw hat
    with wax flowers,
Holding a varnished cane with both hands against her
    spent knees
As she sits alone on the bench, yes oddly
Alone and at rest:

An older wealthier lady, gesticulating and overdressed,
Puffily reciting the liturgy of vexations
To her beautiful companion,
The remote and attractive demi-Parnassian
Whose dark hair catches the sunlight as she listens
With averted face and apparent understanding:

A boy with his crutches laid against the wall
Pale in the shadow where the hops hang over
In light green bundles;—is he, too, waiting
For one who perhaps
Prefers another?
And I, forgetting my khaki, my crude trade,
And the longing that has vexed and silenced me all
    the day,
Now simply consider the quiet people,
How their pattern emerges as the evening kindles
Till the park is a maze of diagonal lines, ah far
Too fine to catch the sun like the glittering webs
The spiders have folded and flung from the fading
    privet.

Only the children, passionately,
Snap my drifting lines with laughter
As they chase each other among the benches
In and out of the dreaming gardens.

To Edward Thomas

(On visiting the memorial stone above Steep in Hampshire)

I

On the way up from Sheet I met some children
Filling a pram with brushwood; higher still
Beside Steep church an old man pointed out
A rough white stone upon a flinty spur
Projecting from the high autumnal woods . . .
I doubt if much has changed since you came here
On your last leave; except the stone; it bears
Your name and trade: 'To Edward Thomas, Poet'.

II

Climbing the steep path through the copse I knew
My cares weighed heavily as yours, my gift
Much less, my hope
No more than yours.
And like you I felt sensitive and somehow apart,
Lonely and exalted by the friendship of the wind
And the placid afternoon enfolding
The dangerous future and the smile.

III

I sat and watched the dusky berried ridge
Of yew-trees, deepened by oblique dark shafts,
Throw back the flame of red and gold and russet
That leapt from beech and ash to birch and chestnut
Along the downward arc of the hill's shoulder,
And sunlight with discerning fingers
Softly explore the distant wooded acres,
Touching the farmsteads one by one with lightness
Until it reached the Downs, whose soft green pastures
Went slanting sea- and skywards to the limits
Where sight surrenders and the mind alone
Can find the sheeps' tracks and the grazing.

And for that moment Life appeared
As gentle as the view I gazed upon.

IV

Later, a whole day later, I remembered
This war and yours and your weary
Circle of failure and your striving
To make articulate the groping voices
Of snow and rain and dripping branches
And love that ailing in itself cried out
About the straggling eaves and ringed the candle
With shadows slouching round your buried head;
And in the lonely house there was no ease
For you, or Helen, or those small perplexed
Children of yours who only wished to please.

Divining this, I knew the voice that called you
Was soft and neutral as the sky
Breathing on the grey horizon, stronger
Than night's immediate grasp, the limbs of mercy
Oblivious as the blood; and growing clearer,
More urgent as all else dissolved away,
—Projected books, half-thoughts, the children's
    birthdays,
And wedding anniversaries as cold
As dates in history—the dream
Emerging from the fact that folds a dream,
The endless rides of stormy-branchèd dark
Whose fibres are a thread within the hand—

Till suddenly, at Arras, you possessed that hinted land.

Post-Script: For Gweno

If I should go away,
Beloved, do not say
'He has forgotten me'.

15

For you abide,
A singing rib within my dreaming side;
You always stay.
And in the mad tormented valley
Where blood and hunger rally
And Death the wild beast is uncaught, untamed,
Our soul withstands the terror
And has its quiet honour
Among the glittering stars your voices named.

from HA! HA! AMONG THE TRUMPETS 1945

Infantry

By day these men ask nothing, and obey;
They eat their bread behind a heap of stones;
Hardship and violence grow an easy way,
Winter is like a girl within their bones.

They learn the gambits of the soul,
Think lightly of the themes of life and death,
All mortal anguish shrunk into an ache
Too nagging to be worth the catch of breath.

Sharing Life's iron rations, marching light,
Enduring to the end the early cold,
The emptiness of noon, the void of night
In whose black market they are bought and sold;
They take their silent stations for the fight
Rum's holy unction makes the dubious bold.

Song

Oh journeyman, Oh journeyman,
Before this endless belt began
Its cruel revolutions, you and she
Naked in Eden shook the apple tree.

Oh soldier lad, Oh soldier lad,
Before the soul of things turned bad,
She offered you so modestly
A shining apple from the tree.

Oh lonely wife, Oh lonely wife,
Before your lover left this life
He took you in his gentle arms.
How trivial then were Life's alarms.

And though Death taps down every street
Familiar as the postman on his beat,
Remember this, Remember this
That Life has trembled in a kiss
From Genesis to Genesis,

And what's transfigured will live on
Long after Death has come and gone.

Goodbye

So we must say Goodbye, my darling,
And go, as lovers go, for ever;
Tonight remains, to pack and fix on labels
And make an end of lying down together.

I put a final shilling in the gas,
And watch you slip your dress below your knees
And lie so still I hear your rustling comb
Modulate the autumn in the trees.

And all the countless things I shall remember
Lay mummy-cloths of silence round my head;
I fill the carafe with a drink of water;
You say 'We paid a guinea for this bed,'

And then, 'We'll leave some gas, a little warmth
For the next resident, and these dry flowers,'
And turn your face away, afraid to speak
The big word, that Eternity is ours.

Your kisses close my eyes and yet you stare
As though God struck a child with nameless fears;
Perhaps the water glitters and discloses
Time's chalice and its limpid useless tears.

Everything we renounce except our selves;
Selfishness is the last of all to go;
Our sighs are exhalations of the earth,
Our footprints leave a track across the snow.

We made the universe to be our home,
Our nostrils took the wind to be our breath,
Our hearts are massive towers of delight,
We stride across the seven seas of death.

Yet when all's done you'll keep the emerald
I placed upon your finger in the street;
And I will keep the patches that you sewed
On my old battledress tonight, my sweet.

Karanje Village

The sweeper said Karanje had a temple
A roof of gold in the gaon:
But I saw only the long-nosed swine and the
        vultures
Groping the refuse for carrion,

And the burial cairns on the hill with its spout
        of dust
Where the mules stamp and graze,
The naked children begging, the elders in poverty,
The sun's dry beat and glaze,

The crumbling hovels like a discredited fortress,
The old hags mumbling by the well,
The young girls in purple always avoiding us,
The monkeys loping obscenely round our smell—

—The trees were obscene with the monkeys' grey
        down-hanging
Their long slow leaping and stare,
The girl in a red sari despairingly swinging her
        rattle,
The sacred monkeys mocking all her care.

And alone by a heap of stones in the lonely salt plain
A little Vishnu of stone,
Silently and eternally simply Being,
Bidding me come alone,

And never entirely turning me away,
But warning me still of the flesh
That catches and limes the singing birds of the soul
And holds their wings in mesh.

But the people are hard and hungry and have no love
Diverse and alien, uncertain in their hate,
Hard stones flung out of Creation's silent matrix,
And the Gods must wait.

And Love must wait, as the unknown yellow poppy
Whose lovely fragile petals are unfurled
Among the lizards in this wasted land.
And when my sweetheart calls me shall I tell her
That I am seeking less and less of world?
And will she understand?

The Mahratta Ghats

The valleys crack and burn, the exhausted plains
Sink their black teeth into the horny veins
Straggling the hills' red thighs, the bleating goats
—Dry bents and bitter thistles in their throats—
Thread the loose rocks by immemorial tracks.
Dark peasants drag the sun upon their backs.

High on the ghat the new turned soil is red,
The sun has ground it to the finest red,
It lies like gold within each horny hand.
Siva has spilt his seed upon this land.

Will she who burns and withers on the plain
Leave, ere too late, her scraggy herds of pain,
The cow-dung fire and the trembling beasts,
The little wicked gods, the grinning priests,
And climb, before a thousand years have fled,
High as the eagle to her mountain bed
Whose soil is fine as flour and blood-red?

But no! She cannot move. Each arid patch
Owns the lean folk who plough and scythe and thatch
Its grudging yield and scratch its stubborn stones.
The small gods suck the marrow from their bones.

Who is it climbs the summit of the road?
Only the beggar bumming his dark load.
Who was it cried to see the falling star?
Only the landless soldier lost in war.

And did a thousand years go by in vain?
And does another thousand start again?

Water Music

Deep in the heart of the lake
Where the last light is clinging
A strange foreboding voice
Is patiently singing.

Do not fear to venture
Where the last light trembles
Because you were in love.
Love never dissembles.

Fear no more the boast, the bully,
The lies, the vain labour.
Make no show for death
As for a rich neighbour.

What stays of the great religions?
An old priest, an old birth.
What stays of the great battles?
Dust on the earth.

Cold is the lake water
And dark as history.
Hurry not and fear not
This oldest mystery.

This strange voice singing,
This slow deep drag of the lake,
This yearning, yearning, this ending
Of the heart and its ache.

The Peasants

The dwarf barefooted, chanting
Behind the oxen by the lake,
Stepping lightly and lazily among the thorntrees
Dusky and dazed with sunlight, half awake;

The women breaking stones upon the highway,
Walking erect with burdens on their heads,
One body growing in another body,
Creation touching verminous straw beds.

Across scorched hills and trampled crops
The soldiers straggle by.
History staggers in their wake.
The peasants watch them die.

Keith Douglas

from COLLECTED POEMS 1951

Time Eating

Ravenous Time has flowers for his food
in Autumn, yet can cleverly make good
each petal: devours animals and men,
but for ten dead he can create ten.

If you enquire how secretly you've come
to mansize from the smallness of a stone
it will appear his effort made you rise
so gradually to your proper size.

But as he makes he eats; the very part
where he began, even the elusive heart,
Time's ruminative tongue will wash
and slow juice masticate all flesh.

That volatile huge intestine holds
material and abstract in its folds:
thought and ambition melt and even the world
will alter, in that catholic belly curled.

But Time, who ate my love, you cannot make
such another; you who can remake
the lizard's tail and the bright snakeskin
cannot, cannot. That you gobbled in
too quick, and though you brought me from a boy
you can make no more of me, only destroy.

The Marvel

A baron of the sea, the great tropic
swordfish, spreadeagled on the thirsty deck
where sailors killed him, in the bright Pacific,

yielded to the sharp enquiring blade
the eye which guided him and found his prey
in the dim place where he was lord.

Which is an instrument forged in semi-darkness;
yet taken from the corpse of this strong traveller
becomes a powerful enlarging glass

10 reflecting the unusual sun's heat.
With it a sailor writes on the hot wood
the name of a harlot in his last port.

For it is one most curious device
of many, kept by the interesting waves,
for I suppose the querulous soft voice

of mariners who rotted into ghosts
digested by the gluttonous tides
could recount many. Let them be your hosts

and take you where these forgotten ships lie
20 with fishes going over the tall masts—
all this emerges from the burning eye.

And to engrave that word the sun goes through
with the power of the sea
writing her name and a marvel too.

Simplify me when I'm Dead

Remember me when I am dead
and simplify me when I'm dead.

As the processes of earth
strip off the colour and the skin:
take the brown hair and blue eye

and leave me simpler than at birth,
when hairless I came howling in
as the moon entered the cold sky.

Of my skeleton perhaps,
so stripped, a learned man will say
'He was of such a type and intelligence,'
    no more.

Thus when in a year collapse
particular memories, you may
deduce, from the long pain I bore

the opinions I held, who was my foe
and what I left, even my appearance
but incidents will be no guide.

Time's wrong-way telescope will show
a minute man ten years hence
and by distance simplified.

Through that lens see if I seem
substance or nothing: of the world
deserving mention or charitable oblivion,

not by momentary spleen
or love into decision hurled,
leisurely arrive at an opinion.

Remember me when I am dead
and simplify me when I'm dead.

Egyptian Sentry, Corniche, Alexandria

Sweat lines the statue of a face
he has; he looks at the sea
and does not smell its animal smell
does not suspect the heaven or hell
in the mind of a passer-by:
sees the moon shining on a place

in the sea, leans on the railing, rests
a hot hand on the eared rifle-muzzle,
nodding to the monotone of his song
10   his tarbush with its khaki cover on.
There is no pain, no pleasure, life's no puzzle
but a standing, a leaning, a sleep between the coasts

of birth and dying. From mother's shoulder
to crawling in the rich gutter, millionaire of smells,
standing, leaning at last with seizing limbs
into the gutter again, while the world swims
on stinks and noises past the filthy wall
and death lifts him to the bearer's shoulder.

The moon shines on the modern flats
20   where sentient lovers or rich couples
lie loving or sleeping after eating.
In the town the cafés and cabarets seating
gossipers, soldiers, drunkards, supple
women of the town, shut out the moon with slats.

Everywhere is a real or artificial race
of life, a struggle of everyone to be
master or mistress of some hour.
But of this no scent or sound reaches him there.
He leans and looks at the sea:
30   sweat lines the statue of a face.

Behaviour of Fish in an Egyptian Tea Garden

As a white stone draws down the fish
she on the seafloor of the afternoon
draws down men's glances and their cruel wish
for love. Slyly red lip on the spoon

slips in a morsel of ice-cream; her hands
white as a milky stone, white submarine
fronds, sink with spread fingers, lean
along the table, carmined at the ends.

A cotton magnate, an important fish
with great eyepouches and a golden mouth
through the frail reefs of furniture swims out
and idling, suspended, stays to watch.

A crustacean old man clamped to his chair
sits coldly near her and might see
her charms through fissures where the eyes
  should be
or else his teeth are parted in a stare.

Captain on leave, a lean dark mackerel,
lies in the offing; turns himself and looks
through currents of sound. The flat-eyed
  flatfish sucks
on a straw, staring from its repose, laxly.

And gallants in shoals swim up and lag,
circling and passing near the white attraction;
sometimes pausing, opening a conversation;
fish pause so to nibble or tug.

Now the ice-cream is finished, is
paid for. The fish swim off on business
and she sits alone at the table, a white stone
unless except to a collector, a rich man.

Cairo Jag

Shall I get drunk or cut myself a piece of cake,
a pasty Syrian with a few words of English
or the Turk who says she is a princess—she dances
apparently by levitation? Or Marcelle, Parisienne
always preoccupied with her dull dead lover:
she has all the photographs and his letters
tied in a bundle and stamped *Décédé* in mauve ink.
All this takes place in a stink of jasmin.

But there are the streets dedicated to sleep
stenches and sour smells, the sour cries
do not disturb their application to slumber
all day, scattered on the pavement like rags
afflicted with fatalism and hashish. The women
offering their children brown-paper breasts
dry and twisted, elongated like the skull,
Holbein's signature. But this stained white town
is something in accordance with mundane conventions—
Marcelle drops her Gallic airs and tragedy
suddenly shrieks in Arabic about the fare
with the cabman, links herself so
with the somnambulists and legless beggars:
it is all one, all as you have heard.

But by a day's travelling you reach a new world
the vegetation is of iron
dead tanks, gun barrels split like celery
the metal brambles have no flowers or berries
and there are all sorts of manure, you can imagine
the dead themselves, their boots, clothes and possessions
clinging to the ground, a man with no head
has a packet of chocolate and a souvenir of Tripoli.

10

20

30

28

Vergissmeinicht

Three weeks gone and the combatants gone,
returning over the nightmare ground
we found the place again, and found
the soldier sprawling in the sun.

The frowning barrel of his gun
overshadowing. As we came on
that day, he hit my tank with one
like the entry of a demon.

Look. Here is the gunpit spoil
the dishonoured picture of his girl
who has put: *Steffi. Vergissmeinicht*
in a copybook gothic script.

We see him almost with content
abased, and seeming to have paid
and mocked at by his own equipment
that's hard and good when he's decayed.

But she would weep to see to-day
how on his skin the swart flies move;
the dust upon the paper eye
and the burst stomach like a cave.

For here the lover and killer are mingled
who had one body and one heart.
And death who had the soldier singled
has done the lover mortal hurt.

I Listen to the Desert Wind

I listen to the desert wind
that will not blow her from my mind;
the stars will not put down a hand,
the moon's ignorant of my wound

moving negligently across
by clouds and cruel tracts of space
as in my brain by nights and days
moves the reflection of her face.

1 0
Skims like a bird my sleepless eye
the sands who at this hour deny
the violent heat they have by day
as she denies her former way:

all the elements agree
with her, to have no sympathy
for my tactless misery
as wonderful and hard as she.

O turn in the dark bed again
and give to him what once was mine
and I'll turn as you turn
2 0
and kiss my swarthy mistress pain.

How to Kill

Under the parabola of a ball,
a child turning into a man,
I looked into the air too long.
The ball fell in my hand, it sang
in the closed fist: *Open Open*
Behold a gift designed to kill.

Now in my dial of glass appears
the soldier who is going to die.
He smiles, and moves about in ways
1 0
his mother knows, habits of his.
The wires touch his face: I cry
NOW. Death, like a familiar, hears

and look, has made a man of dust
of a man of flesh. This sorcery
I do. Being damned, I am amused
to see the centre of love diffused
and the waves of love travel into vacancy.
How easy it is to make a ghost.

The weightless mosquito touches
20   her tiny shadow on the stone,
and with how like, how infinite
a lightness, man and shadow meet.
They fuse. A shadow is a man
when the mosquito death approaches.

Enfidaville

In the church fallen like dancers
lie the Virgin and St Thérèse
on little pillows of dust.
The detonations of the last few days
tore down the ornamental plasters
shivered the hands of Christ.

The men and women who moved like candles
in and out of the houses and the streets
are all gone. The white houses are bare
10   black cages. No one is left to greet
the ghosts tugging at doorhandles
opening doors that are not there.

Now the daylight coming in from the fields
like a labourer, tired and sad,
is peering about among the wreckage, goes
past some corners as though with averted head
not looking at the pain this town holds,
seeing no one move behind the windows.

But already they are coming back; to search
like ants, poking in the débris, finding in it
a bed or a piano and carrying it out.
Who would not love them at this minute?
I seem again to meet
The blue eyes of the images in the church.

Aristocrats

"*I think I am becoming a God*"

The noble horse with courage in his eye
clean in the bone, looks up at a shellburst:
away fly the images of the shires
but he puts the pipe back in his mouth.

Peter was unfortunately killed by an 88:
it took his leg away, he died in the ambulance.
I saw him crawling on the sand; he said
It's most unfair, they've shot my foot off.

How can I live among this gentle
obsolescent breed of heroes, and not weep?
Unicorns, almost,
for they are falling into two legends
in which their stupidity and chivalry
are celebrated. Each, fool and hero, will be an immortal.

The plains were their cricket pitch
and in the mountains the tremendous drop fences
brought down some of the runners. Here then
under the stones and earth they dispose themselves,
I think with their famous unconcern.
It is not gunfire I hear but a hunting horn.

On a Return from Egypt

To stand here in the wings of Europe
disheartened, I have come away
from the sick land where in the sun lay
the gentle sloe-eyed murderers
of themselves, exquisites under a curse;
here to exercise my depleted fury.

For the heart is a coal, growing colder
when jewelled cerulean seas change
into grey rocks, grey water-fringe,
sea and sky altering like a cloth
till colour and sheen are gone both:
cold is an opiate of the soldier.

And all my endeavours are unlucky explorers
come back, abandoning the expedition;
the specimens, the lilies of ambition
still spring in their climate, still unpicked:
but time, time is all I lacked
to find them, as the great collectors before me.

The next month, then, is a window
and with a crash I'll split the glass.
Behind it stands one I must kiss,
person of love or death
a person or a wraith,
I fear what I shall find.

Sidney Keyes

from THE COLLECTED POEMS 1945

Advice for a Journey

I

The drums mutter for war and soon we must begin ˎ
To seek the country where they say that joyˏ
Springs flowerlike among the rocks, to win
The fabulous golden mountain of our peace.

O my friends, we are too young
For explorers, have no skill nor compass,
Nor even that iron certitude which swung
Our fathers at their self-fulfilling North.

So take no rations, remember not your homes
Only the blind and stubborn hope to track
This wilderness. The thoughtful leave their bones
In windy foodless meadows of despair.

Never look back, nor too far forward search
For the white Everest of your desire;
The screes roll underfoot and you will never reach
Those brittle peaks which only clouds may walk.

Others have come before you. The immortal
Live like reflections and their frozen faces
Will give you courage to ignore the subtle
Sneer of the gentian and the iceworn pebble.

10

20

The fifes cry death and the sharp winds call.
Set your face to the rock; go on, go out
Into the bad lands of battle, into the cloud-wall
Of the future, my friends, and leave your fear.

Go forth, my friends, the raven is no sibyl;
Break the clouds' anger with your unchanged faces.
You'll find, maybe, the dream under the hill—
But never Canaan, nor any golden mountain.

Europe's Prisoners

Never a day, never a day passes
But I remember them, their stoneblind faces
Beaten by arclights, their eyes turned inward
Seeking an answer and their passage homeward:

For being citizens of time, they never
Would learn the body's nationality.
Tortured for years now, they refuse to sever
Spirit from flesh or accept our callow century.

Not without hope, but lacking present solace,
The preacher knows the feel of nails and grace;
The singer snores; the orator's facile hands
Are fixed in a gesture no one understands.

Others escaped, yet paid for their betrayal:
Even the politicians with their stale
Visions and cheap flirtation with the past
Will not die any easier at the last.

The ones who took to garrets and consumption
In foreign cities, found a deeper dungeon
Than any Dachau. Free but still confined
The human lack of pity split their mind.

Whatever days, whatever seasons pass,
The prisoners must stare in pain's white face:
Until at last the courage they have learned
Shall burst the walls and overturn the world.

Troll Kings

O wake them not, the big-boned kings,
The sleepers and the sworded kings; the lonely
Inhuman kings who sit with drawn-up knees
Waiting with twisted eyes the time of terror.
O wake them not, the troll kings, the forgotten.

Seraphion the sleeper turns a tired
Metallic eyeball through the lacunae
Of the black tomb; and Arthur mumbles
The names of white-haired women, Guenever
Remembers, and her exhumation, bursting
Like a deep-buried mine on Avalon's touchy climate;
Lancelot too, the double lover, sees him
Riding the roads but rusty now his manners
And gaunt the horse, and white the horse he rides;
And the neurotic banners, and the guessed-at
Grail that was white and gracious as his hope.

Ragnar sleeps too, the great-sworded
King of the trolls, his language no more spoken
Now in the woods, except by winking squirrel
And furtive jay; lies battened
Under black rocks unknown to mole or miner.
Ragnar the ironmaster, O remember
Ragnar regretting the plump peasant girls
Who knew his kingdom and forgot the light.
So sleep the old troll kings, with Barbarossa
Who died on the sharp ice; with Attila
The Tartar buried in a northern forest;
With Alexander, the cold fugitive
From fame and politics; with all outmoded heroes.

O do not speak to them lest they rise up
One cold night under the moon to fight for us.
They wait a backward day: how should they know
Such folly as we suffer, such perplexity
Of soul, such deadly love, such wonder?
Then let them sleep, the poor things, this cold night.

The Expected Guest

The table is spread, the lamp glitters and sighs;
Light on my eyes, light on the high curved iris
And springing from glaze to steel, from cup to knife
Makes sacramental my poor midnight table,
My broken scraps the pieces of a god.

O when they bore you down, the grinning soldiers,
Was it their white teeth you could not forget?
And when you met the beast in the myrtle wood,
When the spear broke and the blood broke out on
        your side,
What Syrian Veronica above you
Stooped with her flaxen cloth as yet unsigned?
And either way, how could you call your darling
To drink the cup of blood your father filled?

We are dying tonight, you in the agèd darkness
and I in the white room my pride has rented.
And either way, we have to die alone.

The laid table stands hard and white as tomorrow.
The lamp sings. The West wind jostles the door.
Though broken the bread, the brain, the brave body
There cannot now be any hope of changing
The leavings to living bone, the bone to bread:
For bladed centuries are drawn between us.
The room is ready, but the guest is dead.

37

The Wilderness

The red rock wilderness
Shall be my dwelling-place.

Where the wind saws at the bluffs
And the pebble falls like thunder
I shall watch the clawed sun
Tear the rocks asunder.

The seven-branched cactus
Will never sweat wine:
My own bleeding feet
Shall furnish the sign.

The rock says 'Endure.'
The wind says 'Pursue.'
The sun says 'I will suck your bones
And afterwards bury you.'

II

Here where the horned skulls mark the limit
Of instinct and intransigeant desire
I beat against the rough-tongued wind
Towards the heart of fire.

So knowing my youth, which was yesterday,
And my pride which shall be gone tomorrow,
I turn my face to the sun, remembering gardens
Planted by others—Longinus, Guillaume de
        Lorris
And all love's gardeners, in an early May.
O sing, small ancient bird, for I am going
Into the sun's garden, the red rock desert
I have dreamt of and desired more than the lilac's
        promise.
The flowers of the rock shall never fall.

O speak no more of love and death
And speak no word of sorrow:
My anger's eaten up my pride
And both shall die tomorrow.

Knowing I am no lover, but destroyer,
I am content to face the destroying sun.
There shall be no more journeys, nor the anguish
Of meeting and parting, after the last great parting
From the images of dancing and the gardens
Where the brown bird chokes in its song:
Until that last great meeting among mountains
Where the metal bird sings madly from the fire.

O speak no more of ceremony,
Speak no more of fame:
My heart must seek a burning land
To bury its foolish pain.

By the dry river at the desert edge
I regret the speaking rivers I have known;
The sunlight shattered under the dark bridge
And many tongues of rivers in the past.
Rivers and gardens, singing under the willows,
The glowing moon. . .
                                And all the poets of summer
Must lament another spirit's passing over.

O never weep for me, my love,
Or seek me in this land:
But light a candle for my luck
And bear it in your hand.

III

In this hard garden where the earth's ribs
Lie bare from her first agony, I seek
The home of the gold bird, the predatory Phoenix.
O louder than the tongue of any river
Call the red flames among the shapes of rock:

60   And this is my calling . . .
                              Though my love must sit
     Alone with her candle in a darkened room
     Listening to music that is not present or
     Turning a flower in her childish hands
     And though we were a thousand miles apart . . .
     This is my calling, to seek the red rock desert
     And speak for all those who have lost the gardens,
     Forgotten the singing, yet dare not find the desert—
     To sing the song that rises from the fire.
        It is not profitable to remember
70   How my friends fell, my heroes turned to squalling
     Puppets of history; though I would forget
     The way of this one's failure, that one's exile—
     How the small foreign girl
     Grew crazed with her own beauty; how the poet
     Talks to the wall in a deserted city;
     How others danced until the Tartar wind
     Blew in the doors; or sitting alone at midnight
     Heard Solomon Eagle beat his drum in the streets:
     This is the time to ask their pardon
80   For any act of coldness in the past.
     There is no kind of space can separate us:
     No weather, even this cruel sun, can change us;
     No dress, though you in shining satin walk
     Or you in velvet, while I run in tatters
     Against the fiery wind. There is no loss,
     Only the need to forget. This is my calling . . .
        But behind me the rattle of stones underfoot,
     Stones from the bare ridge rolling and skidding:
     A voice I know, but had consigned to silence,
90   Another calling: my own words coming back . . .

        'And I would follow after you
     Though it were a thousand mile:
     Though you crossed the deserts of the world to the
              kingdom of death, my dear,
     I would follow after you and stand beside you there.'

IV

Who is this lady, flirting with the wind,
Blown like a tangle of dried flowers through the desert?
This is my lover whom I left
Alone at evening between the candles—
White fingers nailed with flame—in an empty house.
Here we have come to the last ridge, the river
Crossed and the birds of summer left to silence.
And we go forth, we go forth together
With our lank shadows dogging us, scrambling
Across the raw red stones.
                              There is no parting
From friends, but only from the ways of friendship;
Nor from our lovers, though the forms of love
Change often as the landscape of this journey
To the dark valley where the gold bird burns.
I say, Love is a wilderness and these bones
Proclaim no failure, but the death of youth.
We say, You must be ready for the desert
Even among the orchards starred with blossom,
Even in spring, or at the waking moment
When the man turns to the woman, and both are afraid.
All who would save their life must find the desert—
The lover, the poet, the girl who dreams of Christ,
And the swift runner, crowned with another laurel:
They all must face the sun, the red rock desert,
And see the burning of the metal bird.
Until you have crossed the desert and faced that fire
Love is an evil, a shaking of the hand,
A sick pain draining courage from the heart.

We do not know the end, we cannot tell
That valley's shape, nor whether the white fire
Will blind us instantly . . .
                              Only we go
Forward, we go forward together, leaving
Nothing except a worn-out way of loving.

V

Flesh is fire, the fire of flesh burns white
Through living limbs: a cold fire in the blood.
130   We must learn to live without love's food.

We shall see the sky without birds, the wind
Will blow no leaves, will ruffle no new river.
We shall walk in the desert together.
Flesh is fire, frost and fire.
We have turned in time, we shall see
The Phoenix burning under a rich tree.
Flesh is fire.

Solomon Eagle's drum shall be filled with sand:
The dancers shall wear out their skilful feet,
140   The pretty lady shall be wrapped in a rough sheet.

We go now, but others must follow:
The rivers are drying, the trees are falling,
The red rock wilderness is calling.

And they will find who linger in the garden
The way of time is not a river but
A pilferer who will not ask their pardon.

Flesh is fire, frost and fire:
Flesh is fire in this wilderness of fire
Which is our dwelling.

Henry Reed

from A MAP OF VERONA 1946

The Door and the Window

My love, you are timely come, let me lie by your heart.
For waking in the dark this morning, I woke to that
    mystery,
Which we can all wake to, at some dark time or another:
Waking to find the room not as I thought it was,
But the window further away, and the door in another
    direction.

This was not home, and you were far away,
And I woke sick, and held by another passion,
In the icy grip of a dead, tormenting flame,
Consumed by the night, watched by the door and the
    window,
10   On a bed of stone, waiting for the day to bring you.

The window is sunlit now, the spring day sparkles
    beyond it,
The door has opened: and can you, at last beside me,
Drive under the day that frozen and faithless darkness,
With its unseen torments flickering, which neither
The dearest look nor the longest kiss assuages?

Lives

You cannot cage a field.
You cannot wire it, as you wire a summer's roses
To sell in towns; you cannot cage it
Or kill it utterly. All you can do is to force
Year after year from the stream to the cold woods
The heavy glitter of wheat, till its body tires
And the yield grows weaker and dies. But the field
      never dies,
Though you build on it, burn it black, or domicile
A thousand prisoners upon its empty features.
10   You cannot kill a field. A field will reach
Right under the streams to touch the limbs of its brothers.

But you can cage the woods.
You can throw up fences, as round a recalcitrant heart
Spring up remonstrances. You can always cage the woods,
Hold them completely. Confine them to hill or valley,
You can alter their face, their shape; uprooting their
      outer saplings
You can even alter their wants, and their smallest
      longings
Press to your own desires. The woods succumb
To the paths made through their life, withdraw the trees,
20   Betake themselves where you tell them, and acquiesce.
The woods retreat; their protest of leaves whirls
Pitifully to the cooling heavens, like dead or dying
      prayers.

But what can you do with a stream?
You can widen it here, or deepen it there, but even
If you alter its course entirely it gives the impression
That this is what it always wanted. Moorhens return
To nest or hide in the reeds which quickly grow up there,
The fishes breed in it, stone settles on to stone.
The stream announces its places where the water will
      bubble

Daily and unconcerned, contentedly ruffling and
        scuffling
With the drifting sky or the leaf. Whatever you do,
A stream has rights, for a stream is always water;
To cross it you have to bridge it; and it will not flow
        uphill.

LESSONS OF THE WAR

(To Alan Mitchell)

1. Naming of Parts

Today we have naming of parts. Yesterday,
We had daily cleaning. And tomorrow morning,
We shall have what to do after firing. But today,
Today we have naming of parts. Japonica
Glistens like coral in all of the neighbouring gardens,
    And today we have naming of parts.

This is the lower sling swivel. And this
Is the upper sling swivel, whose use you will see,
When you are given your slings. And this is the piling
        swivel,
Which in your case you have not got. The branches
Hold in the gardens their silent, eloquest gestures,
    Which in our case we have not got.

This is the safety-catch, which is always released
With an easy flick of the thumb. And please do not let me
See anyone using his finger. You can do it quite easy
If you have any strength in your thumb. The blossoms
Are fragile and motionless, never letting anyone see
    Any of them using their finger.

And this you can see is the bolt. The purpose of this
Is to open the breech, as you see. We can slide it
Rapidly backwards and forwards: we call this
Easing the spring. And rapidly backwards and forwards
The early bees are assaulting and fumbling the flowers:
    They call it easing the Spring.

They call it easing the Spring: it is perfectly easy
If you have any strength in your thumb: like the bolt,
And the breech, and the cocking-piece, and the point of
        balance,
Which in our case we have not got; and the almond-
        blossom
Silent in all of the gardens and the bees going backwards
        and forwards,
    For today we have naming of parts.

2. Judging Distances

Not only how far away, but the way that you say it
Is very important. Perhaps you may never get
The knack of judging a distance, but at least you know
How to report on a landscape: the central sector,
The right of arc and that, which we had last Tuesday,
    And at least you know

That maps are of time, not place, so far as the army
Happens to be concerned—the reason being,
Is one which need not delay us. Again, you know
There are three kinds of tree, three only, the fir and
        the poplar,
And those which have bushy tops to; and lastly
    That things only seem to be things.

A barn is not called a barn, to put it more plainly,
Or a field in the distance, where sheep may be safely
    grazing.

You must never be over-sure. You must say, when
    reporting:
At five o'clock in the central sector is a dozen
Of what appear to be animals; whatever you do,
   Don't call the bleeders *sheep*.

I am sure that's quite clear; and suppose, for the sake
    of example,
20 The one at the end, asleep, endeavours to tell us
What he sees over there to the west, and how far away,
After first having come to attention. There to the west,
On the fields of summer the sun and the shadows bestow
   Vestments of purple and gold.

The still white dwellings are like a mirage in the heat,
And under the swaying elms a man and a woman
Lie gently together. Which is, perhaps, only to say
That there is a row of houses to the left of arc,
And that under some poplars a pair of what appear to be
    humans
30   Appear to be loving.

Well that, for an answer, is what we might rightly call
Moderately satisfactory only, the reason being,
Is that two things have been omitted, and those are
    important.
The human beings, now: in what direction are they,
And how far away, would you say? And do not forget
   There may be dead ground in between.

There may be dead ground in between; and I may not
    have got
The knack of judging a distance; I will only venture
A guess that perhaps between me and the apparent lovers,
40 (Who, incidentally, appear by now to have finished)
At seven o'clock from the houses, is roughly a distance
   Of about one year and a half.

3. Unarmed Combat

In due course of course you will all be issued with
Your proper issue; but until tomorrow,
You can hardly be said to need it; and until that time,
We shall have unarmed combat. I shall teach you.
The various holds and rolls and throws and breakfalls
    Which you may sometimes meet.

And the various holds and rolls and throws and breakfalls
Do not depend on any sort of weapon,
But only on what I might coin a phrase and call
10   The ever-important question of human balance,
And the ever-important need to be in a strong
    Position at the start.

There are many kinds of weakness about the body,
Where you would least expect, like the ball of the foot.
But the various holds and rolls and throws and breakfalls
Will always come in useful. And never be frightened
To tackle from behind: it may not be clean to do so,
    But this is global war.

So give them all you have, and always give them
20   As good as you get; it will always get you somewhere.
(You may not know it, but you can tie a Jerry
Up without a rope; it is one of the things I shall teach you.)
Nothing will matter if only you are ready for him.
    The readiness is all.

The readiness is all. How can I help but feel
I have been here before? But somehow then,
I was the tied-up one. How to get out
Was always then my problem. And even if I had
A piece of rope I was always the sort of person
30   Who threw the rope aside.

A piece of rope I was always the sort of person
Which was never as good as I got, and it got me nowhere.

And the various holds and rolls and throws and breakfalls
Somehow or other I always seemed to put
In the wrong place. And as for war, my wars
    Were global from the start.

Perhaps I was never in a strong position,
Or the ball of my foot got hurt, or I had some weakness
Where I had least expected. But I think I see your point.
While awaiting a proper issue, we must learn the lesson
Of the ever-important question of human balance.
    It is courage that counts.

Things may be the same again; and we must fight
Not in the hope of winning but rather of keeping
Something alive: so that when we meet our end,
It may be said that we tackled wherever we could,
That battle-fit we lived, and though defeated,
    Not without glory fought.

from THE DESERT

3. South

They had seen for a hundred days their shadows on ice.
What suffering god whose image they were made in
Had drawn them curious to his blizzard centre,
    And sent them back?

Who knew? Unanswered, they returned unspeaking
To the brutal coast their dreams had kept familiar,
And came in the last few hours to where a rock
    Rose from the ice.

Careful but unreflecting, they passed across it,
And went their way, save one. He on the rock
Pressed suddenly against the rock for comfort,
    And comfort came.

(Rocks were so rare, one should not pass them by.)
After a time he opened his eyes. Yes, thinking,
'The others? I cannot stay here on a rock for ever',
    He opened his eyes,

And there was a world. He had curved his arms right over
His head, and his cheek pressed hard against the rock,
And all he saw was his fragment of rock, and beyond it,
20   A fraction of sea.

He saw at once it was strange. For so many days,
There had been no place where he might not see the ice,
And the blossoming of ice and snow under visible winds
    From the mountain-range,

Till an ignorant gesture had hidden them utterly.
He watched. The world remained. And the silent bay
And the great black rock passed through his waiting veins
    The shock of peace.

It might be a bay, he thought, on the summer islands,
30   Far in the north. (North? They had once been south.)
'But look more closely', the landscape suddenly told him,
    'What do you see?'

And he saw his life. He saw it, and turned away,
And wept hot tears down the rock's hard cheek, and kissed
Its wrinkled mouths with the kiss of passion, crying,
    'Where is my love?'

'Now? At this moment?' The world broke at his words.
In the little prison the furious prisoner howling
Showed him through glaciers the heat's still unforgotten
40   Knocking of blood.

And showed him too that there would be no return.
His coasts henceforth would calve in change unceasing,
And like a ship, the heart would shake and tack
    To a varying port,

Beneath whose recondite stars another quiet,
Not peace but like it, awaited him now, and held
Its tortured arms of truth to receive its lovers:
    It was the ice.

'Ice will come drifting over our sighs like music,
Now and forever', he whispered, 'And though from sleep,
We wake up weeping, our tears we shall find are frozen,
    As soon as wept.

'And of that we must learn to be glad. Good-bye', he cried,
'Oh delusive rock, we shall not come here again',
And climbing round and down and after the others,
    Faced the full day.

from TINTAGEL

4. Iseult La Belle

Bold in clear weather, or halting through the mist,
I have seen it all, and shall see it again and again:
The taut strained body of Tristram climbing the rocks,
The sunlit fear of Mark in the magic grotto,
The desolate parted lips of that other Iseult
Lost to the language of this dangerous coast.
I am she, the heart and centre of desire,
The well-beloved, the eternally-reappearing
Ghost on the lips of spring.

              And do you expect a face
Calm at the heart of torment? Calmness in me, the fear
Of all the poets who dreaded the passing of beauty,
And called on Time to stay his decaying hand,
And who, in their hearts, dreaded more than beauty's passing,
Its perpetual arrest?

I am that point of arrest;
Though I drop back into oblivion, though I retreat
Into the soft, hoarse chant of the past, the unsoaring, dull
And songless harmony behind the screen of stone,
20   I do not age.
But I come, in whatever season, like a new year,
In such a vision as the open gates reveal
As you saunter into a courtyard, or enter a city,
And inside the city you carry another city,
Inside delight, delight.
And it seems you have borne me always, the love within you,
Under the ice of winter, hidden in darkness.
Winter on winter, frozen and unrevealing,
To flower in a sudden moment, the bloom held high towards
        heaven,
30   Steady in the glowing air the white and gleaming calyx,
Lightness of heart.

So, I am hard to remember,
As summer is hard to remember in the press of winter,
When the waking kiss is a snowflake on the mouth,
The petals lost and forgotten; and, as you move to
        embrace me,
I am that weary face, that fearful rejecting hand,
Which begs for freedom from you.
And under the dark the waves groan again on the rocks,
The hungry ruins divide the mists among them,
40   The land-wind and sea-wind meeting.

Do you expect a heart,
Unmoved, and tears unfallen? Oh, look again:
Am I not yourself as well?
And do I not know the arena of separation,
Encircled and watched by the indifferent fields of corn,
The heavy fountains of trees in the shining heat,
The hillsides and rivers, grasses and level beaches;
Even so close you may touch them with your hand,
They are inaccessible; yet they burn the sense.

And do you think I would not reach towards you,
As the screen of stone falls into place between us,
And the dirge begins, do you think I do not know
That somewhere beyond me, lost, and lost and falling,
(Do you think I do not know?)
That under the droning gales which tear the stones,
When you dare not move a step in the dark which
     surrounds you,
You strive to find some angle of the broken castle,
And tug at the streaming earth to find some spot
In which you may plant your torn chimerical flowers
With a ruined wall to protect them?

O you, who will never be other than children,
Do you think, if I could, I would not reach my hand,
Through the burning mist and the echoing night of
    blackness,
To bless you, soothe you, and guide you through your hell?

Roy Fuller

from THE MIDDLE OF A WAR 1942

Soliloquy in an Air Raid

The will dissolves, the heart becomes excited,
Skull suffers formication; moving words
Fortuitously issue from my hand.
The winter heavens, seen all day alone,
Assume the colour of aircraft over the phthisic
Guns.

But who shall I speak to with this poem?

Something was set between the words and the world
I watched today; perhaps the necrotomy
Of love or the spectre of pretence; a vagueness;
But murdering their commerce like a tariff.

Inside the poets the words are changed to desire,
And formulations of feeling are lost in action
Which hourly transmutes the basis of common speech.
Our dying is effected in the streets,
London an epicentrum; to the stench
And penny prostitution in the shelters
Dare not extend the hospital and bogus
Hands of propaganda.

Ordered this year:
A billion tons of broken glass and rubble,
Blockade of chaos, the other requisites
For the reduction of Europe to a rabble.

Who can observe this save as a frightened child
Or careful diarist? And who who can speak
And still retain the tones of civilization?
The verse that was the speech of observation—
Jonson's cartoon of the infant bourgeoisie,
Shakespeare's immense assertion that man alone
Is almost the equal of his environment,
The Chinese Wall of class round Pope, the Romantic
Denunciation of origin and mould—
Is sunk in the throat between the opposing voices:

*I am the old life, which promises even less
In the future, and guarantees your loss.*

*And I the new, in which your function and
Your form will be dependent on my end.*

Kerensky said of Lenin: *I must kindly* ·
Orientate him to what is going on.
Watching the images of fabulous girls
On cinema screens, the liberal emotion
Of the slightly inhuman poet wells up in me,
As irrelevant as Kerensky. It is goodbye
To the social life which permitted melancholy
And madness in the isolation of its writers,
To a struggle as inconclusive as the Hundred
Years' War. The air, as welcome as morphia,
This 'rich ambiguous aesthetic air'
Which now I breathe, is an effective diet
Only for actors: in the lonely box
The author mumbles to himself, the play
Unfolds spontaneous as the human wish,
As autumn dancing, vermilion on rocks.

Epitaph on a Bombing Victim

Reader, could his limbs be found
Here would lie a common man:
History inflicts no wound
But explodes what it began,
And with its enormous lust
For division splits the dust.
Do not ask his nation; that
Was History's confederate.

The Middle of a War

My photograph already looks historic.
The promising youthful face, the matelot's collar,
Say 'This one is remembered for a lyric.
His place and period—nothing could be duller.'

Its position is already indicated—
The son or brother in the album; pained
The expression and the garments dated,
His fate so obviously preordained.

The original turns away: as horrible thoughts,
Loud fluttering aircraft slope above his head
At dusk. The ridiculous empires break like biscuits.
Ah, life has been abandoned by the boats—
Only the trodden island and the dead
Remain, and the once inestimable caskets.

Y.M.C.A. Writing Room

A map of the world is on the wall: its lying
Order and compression shadow these bent heads.
Here we try to preserve communications;
The maps mock us with dangerous blues and reds.

Today my friends were drafted; they are about
To be exploded, to be scattered over
That coloured square which in reality
Is a series of scenes, is boredom, cover,

Nostalgia, labour, death. They will explore
Minutely particular deserts, seas and reefs,
Invest a thousand backcloths with their moods,
And all will carry, like a cancer, grief.

In England at this moment the skies contain
Ellipses of birds within their infinite planes,
At night the ragged patterns of the stars;
And distant trees are like the branching veins

Of an anatomical chart: as menacing
As pistols the levelled twigs present their buds.
They have exchanged for this illusion of danger
The ordeal of walking in the sacred wood.

The season cannot warm them nor art console.
These words are false as the returning Spring
From which this March history has made subtraction:
The spirit has gone and left the marble thing.

Harbour Ferry

The oldest and simplest thoughts
Rise with the antique moon:
How she enamels men
And artillery under her sphere,
Eyelids and hair and throats
Rigid in love and war;
How this has happened before.

And how the lonely man
Raises his head and shudders
With a brilliant sense of the madness,

57

The age and shape of his planet,
Wherever his human hand,
Whatever his set of tenets,
The long and crucial minute.

Tonight the moon has risen
Over a quiet harbour,
Through twisted iron and labour,
Lighting the half-drowned ships.
Oh surely the fatal chasm
Is closer, the furious steps
Swifter? The silver drips

From the angle of the wake:
The moon is flooding the faces.
The moment is over: the forces
Controlling lion nature
Look out of the eyes and speak:
Can you believe in a future
Left only to rock and creature?

from A LOST SEASON 1944

In Africa

Parabolas of grief, the hills are never
Hills and the plains,
Where through the torrid air the lions shiver,
No longer plains.

Just as the lives of lions now are made
Shabby with rifles,
This great geography shrinks into sad
And personal trifles.

For those who are in love and are exiled
Can never discover
How to be happy: looking upon the wild
They see for ever

The cultivated acre of their pain;
The clouds like dreams,
Involved, improbable; the endless plain
Precisely as it seems.

The Green Hills of Africa

The green, humped, wrinkled hills: with such a look
Of age (or youth) as to erect the hair.
They crouch above the ports or on the plain,
Beneath the matchless skies; are like a strange
Girl's shoulders suddenly against your hands.
What covers them so softly, vividly?
They break at the sea in a cliff, a mouth of red:
Upon the plain are unapproachable,
Furrowed and huge, dramatically lit.

And yet one cannot be surprised at what
The hills contain. The girls run up the slope,
Their oiled and shaven heads like caramels.
Behind, the village, with its corrugated
Iron, the wicked habit of the store.
The villagers cough, the sacking blows from the naked
Skin of a child, a white scum on his lips.
The youths come down in feathers from the peak.
And over all a massive frescoed sky.

The poisoner proceeds by tiny doses,
The victim weaker and weaker but uncomplaining.
Soon they will only dance for money, will
Discover more and more things can be sold.

What gods did you expect to find here, with
What healing powers? What subtle ways of life?
No, there is nothing but the forms and colours,
And the emotion brought from a world already
Dying of what starts to infect the hills.

The Giraffes

I think before they saw me the giraffes
Were watching me. Over the golden grass,
The bush and ragged open tree of thorn,
From a grotesque height, under their lightish horns,
Their eyes were fixed on mine as I approached them.
The hills behind descended steeply: iron-
Coloured outcroppings of rock half covered by
Dull green and sepia vegetation, dry
And sunlit: and above, the piercing blue
10   Where clouds like islands lay or like swans flew.

Seen from those hills the scrubby plain is like
A large-scale map whose features have a look
Half menacing, half familiar, and across
Its brightness arms of shadow ceaselessly
Revolve. Like small forked twigs or insects move
Giraffes, upon the great map where they live.

When I went nearer, their long bovine tails
Flicked loosely, and deliberately they turned,
An undulation of dappled grey and brown,
20   And stood in profile with those curious planes
Of neck and sloping haunches. Just as when,
Quite motionless, they watched I never thought
Them moved by fear, a wish to be a tree,
So as they put more ground between us I
Saw evidence that these were animals
With no desire for intercourse, or no
Capacity.

Above the falling sun,
Like visible winds the clouds are streaked and spun,
And cold and dark now bring the image of
30   Those creatures walking without pain or love.

The Plains

The only blossoms of the plains are black
And rubbery, the spiked spheres of the thorn,
And stuffed with ants. It is before the rains;
The stream is parched to pools, occasional
And green, where tortoise flop; the birds are songless;
Towers of whirling dust glide past like ghosts.
But in the brilliant sun, against the sky,
The river coarse is vivid and the grass
Flaxen: the strong striped haunches of the zebra,
10   The white fawn black, like flags, of the gazelles,
Move as emotions or as kindly actions.
The world is nothing but a fairy tale
Where everything is beautiful and good.

At night the stars were faint, the plateau chill;
The great herds gathered, were invisible,
And coughed and made inarticulate noises
Of fear and yearning: sounds of their many hooves
Came thudding quietly. The headlights caught
Eyes and the pallid racing forms. I thought
20   Of nothing but the word *humanity*:
And I was there outside the square of warmth,
In darkness, in the crowds and padding, crying.
Suddenly the creamy shafts of light
Revealed the lion. Slowly it swung its great
Maned head, then—loose, suède, yellow—loped away.
O purposeful and unapproachable!
Then later his repugnant hangers-on:
A pair of squint hyenas limping past.

This awful ceremony of the doomed, unknown
30   And innocent victim has its replicas
Embedded in our memories and in
Our history. The archetypal myths
Stirred in my mind.
                              The next day, over all,
The sun was flooding and the sky rose tall.
Where rock had weathered through the soil I saw
A jackal running, barking, turning his head.
Four vultures sat upon the rock and pecked,
And when I neared them flew away on wings
Like hair. They left a purple scrap of skin.
40   Have I discovered all the plains can show?
The animals gallop, spring, are beautiful,
And at the end of every day is night.

Askari's Song

At dusk when the sky is pale,
Across a three years' journey
I can see the far white hill
Which in my land is like a
Conscience or maker.

At dusk when cattle cross
The red dust of the roadway,
I smell the sweetish grass,
Half animal, half flowers,
10   Which also is ours.

At dusk the roads along
The separating plains are
So sad with our deep song
I could expect the mountain
To drift like a fountain,

And, conquering time, our tribe
Out of the dust to meet us
Come happy, free, alive,
Bringing the snow-capped boulder

Over their shoulder.

What is Terrible

Life at last I know is terrible:
The innocent scene, the innocent walls and light
And hills for me are like the cavities
Of surgery or dreams. The visible might
Vanish, for all it reassures, in white.

This apprehension has come slowly to me,
Like symptoms and bulletins of sickness. I
Must first be moved across two oceans, then
Bored, systematically and sickeningly,

In a place where war is news. And constantly

I must be threatened with what is certainly worse:
Peril and death, but no less boring. And
What else? Besides my fear, my misspent time,
My love, hurt and postponed, there is the hand
Moving the empty glove; the bland

Aspect of nothing disguised as something; that
Part of living incommunicable,
For which we try to find vague adequate
Images, and which, after all,

Is quite surprisingly communicable.

Because in the clear hard light of war the ghosts
Are seen to be suspended by wires, and in
The old house the attic is empty: and the furious
Inner existence of objects and even
Ourselves is largely a myth: and for the sin

To blame our fathers, to attribute vengeance
To the pursuing chorus, and to live
In a good and tenuous world of private values,
Is simply to lie when only truth can give
Continuation in time to bread and love.

For what is terrible is the obvious
Organization of life: the oiled black gun,
And what it cost, the destruction of Europe by
Its councils; the unending justification
Of that which cannot be justified, what is done.

The year, the month, the day, the minute, at war
Is terrible and my participation
And that of all the world is terrible.
My living now must bear the laceration
Of the herd, and always will. What's done

To me is done to many. I can see
No ghosts, but only the fearful actual
Lives of my comrades. If the empty whitish
Horror is ever to be flushed and real,
It must be for them and changed by them all.

During a Bombardment by V-Weapons

The little noises of the house:
Drippings between the slates and ceiling;
From the electric fire's cooling,
Tickings; the dry feet of a mouse:

These at the ending of a war
Have power to alarm me more
Than the ridiculous detonations
Outside the gently coughing curtains.

And, love, I see your pallor bears
A far more pointed threat than steel.
Now all the permanent and real
Furies are settling in upstairs.

PART TWO

Poets of the Aftermath

INTRODUCTION

For a variety of reasons, the end of hostilities brought with it a decided change in the climate for poetry. There was a marked slackening of interest in poetry generally, partly because there was no longer any shortage of suitable reading matter, and partly because there were many other more pressing matters calling for attention in the postwar scramble for demobilisation, housing, employment, rehabilitation, and better living conditions than had been known before the war. It might be said that, to some extent, the war had served to simplify attitudes during the 1939–45 period. For with practically the whole population united in activities concentrated, in the initial stages, on the fight for survival and, later, upon total victory over enemy forces, danger and deprivation had heightened, and given a national sense of purpose to, ordinary experience, so that poetry seemed an appropriate outlet. With the end of the fighting those who had survived the blitz (German bombing raids) of the towns and cities, and the younger men and women returning from service with the Forces wished alike to resume normal living and to forget the years of war.

The emphasis of the wartime slogan 'We're all in it together' was suddenly switched to all the possibilities of the 'New Britain for a better world', about which so much had been heard in the classes and publications of the Army Bureau of Current Affairs. In 1942, at the request of the Coalition Government, Sir William Beveridge had conducted a survey of social insurance and, in his Report, had put forth specific proposals for the elimination of the 'Five Great Evils ... Want, Disease, Ignorance, Squalor and Idleness', by means of a comprehensive system of national insurance which provided for a free health service, children's allowances, and full employment. Unlike most government publications, the Beveridge Report was widely read and received the general approval of both civilians and servicemen. The provisions, and the principles behind them, were hotly debated whenever the future was discussed. The demand for this social document went far beyond all expectations, even from units on active service. Clearly Beveridge had sensed and brought out into the open what had long been felt as a primary human need by a major part of the population, and before long the Beveridge Report assumed, for ordinary people at least, all the proportions of a Statement of War Aims, implying that the struggle was not only against the Nazis but also against the social injustices of the past. Whether the Government had authorised the issue of the document as a genuine sign of its intentions or as psychological propaganda aimed at reinforcing morale, may never be known; certainly there appeared to be some second thoughts about the wisdom of making the document so widely available. For instance, when the Army Bureau of Current Affairs produced a pamphlet outlining and examining the Beveridge proposals, the interest it aroused seemed to take the authorities by surprise and instructions were given for its withdrawal, but the objections throughout the Services were strong enough to compel its reissue. During the war years, then, a social revolution had been quietly taking place which was to have far-reaching effects. Young men and women came back home better informed, more experienced, and in many cases more determined to insist upon much-needed social reforms. It was in this mood that, on the strength of the Labour Party's manifesto, *Let us Face the Future*, with its wholesale commitment to the Beveridge proposals, that the people (many of them voting for the first time) elected a Labour Government with an overwhelming majority in July 1945. 'This is the dawn of a new day and in the light of it we are going to march forward to those things of which we have dreamed for years past,' announced the new Minister of Labour, George Isaacs. Not that the politicians were greatly trusted by electors mindful of 'earlier betrayals' and easily made election promises. In an article entitled 'The Obsolete Political Mind', Derek Stanford portrayed the professional politician as a creature of expedience and diplomacy rather than of moral standards and, voicing the apprehensions of many, called for 'the formation of committees among the electorate who would scrutinise the behaviour of their representatives and call them to answer for their conduct'.

By 1946 the wartime boom in poetry had spent itself. Apart

from the work of well-established poets whose reputations were secure, there was so little demand for poetry that publishers were refusing even to consider the work of younger and unestablished poets. The rising cost of living and inflationary trends made the situation even more difficult for young poets. Indeed, by 1950 the position had deteriorated so much that the International P.E.N. held a much publicised meeting to consider 'The Crisis in Poetry' and to do what it could to correct 'a situation which, if it continues and develops, may have a serious effect upon the great stream of English poetry'. This may explain why the initiative in poetry seemed for a few years to pass to older poets such as Edith Sitwell and Edwin Muir, or those who had not served in the Forces, such as Dylan Thomas and Norman Nicholson.

It may also explain why so little was published by the younger poets which recorded or reflected the conditions in which they lived, or which examined the implications of the extraordinary changes taking place both inside and outside the British Isles. For, after all, this was the period in which the Welfare State was established in Britain; in which the War Crimes Tribunal at Nuremberg revealed horrors of the concentration camps which had only been rumoured before, and impressed the monstrous images of Auschwitz, Belsen, Buchenwald and Dachau upon the minds of all sensitive and thoughtful people; in which the famine conditions on the continent provoked Victor Gollancz to launch his 'Save Europe Now' campaign, and thousands of food-rationed Britons sent food parcels to the German people; in which India, Ceylon, Burma and Pakistan were given independence and the concept of the multiracial Commonwealth replaced that of the British Empire; and in which the iron curtain fell, effectively dividing Europe into two armed camps.

Perhaps more to the point is the fact that they were living under the shadow of the Bomb (on 5 August the first atomic bomb was dropped on Hiroshima—the Japanese surrender followed on 15 August), and trying to come to terms with the reality of a situation in which civilisation could easily destroy itself. As Paul Dehn, one of the few young poets to write directly about the atomic bomb and its significance for mankind, expressed it in a poem entitled 'Thirty-Five':

In the end and the beginning was the Word
Which made and shall unmake all. But not until now,
On the middle night of my life at the dead moon's rising,
Not since the voice of One
Moved on the bucking waters like a bird,
Dividing light from darkness, improvising
Star, mayfly, wood-anemone and Man,
Has Man been driven to measure his own time
On Earth against the days of Earth itself;
Or, scanning the finite and the infinite gulf,
Feared them to be the same.

When in September 1949 the news broke that the U.S.S.R. had developed its own atomic bomb and in response President Truman informed the world that the U.S.A. intended to manufacture the hydrogen bomb, annihilation by nuclear warfare seemed not too remote a possibility.

What could poetry say that public events had not already made abundantly clear? For many poets there seemed to be no recognisable pattern of values by which to integrate their experience of both inner and outer worlds. It is not surprising that some poets confined themselves to finding a personal solution to their own problems; or that others, in circumstances so unfavourable to the publication of poetry, were struggling desperately just to make their voices heard. If there were no dominating groups or schools during the period, it is nevertheless possible to distinguish three major trends which exercised a strong influence on what was written. First, one can hardly miss the continuing strain of neo-romanticism, shown perhaps at its best in the later poems of Dylan Thomas. Secondly, there was a marked tendency for poets to become increasingly preoccupied with religious and metaphysical subjects (almost as if the poets concerned were intent on renewing or discovering a faith within themselves), approaching at points the Christian existentialism of Kierkegaard, Marcel and Jaspers, and making great use of archetypal imagery—as can be seen in the work of Edith Sitwell, Edwin Muir, David Gascoyne, Norman Nicholson, Kathleen Raine, Anne Ridler and Vernon Watkins. Thirdly, there were various regional and nationalistic tendencies, notably in Wales, Scotland and Ireland, or in the work of such individual poets as Norman Nicholson, Vernon Watkins and R. S. Thomas.

Although Dame EDITH SITWELL published her first collection of verse in 1915 and edited an anthology, *Wheels*, during the days of the First World War, her extraordinary talent was for many years obscured by the sensational methods by which she and her brothers, Sir Osbert and Sacheverell, adopted in making themselves known, and in attacking all those not in sympathy with their poetry, their ideas or their manner of presenting them. Consequently, Dame Edith's work failed to receive the serious attention it deserved. Even that discerning critic, Dr F. R. Leavis, failed to appreciate the purpose of her experiments. 'The Sitwells', he wrote in 1932, 'belong to the history of publicity rather than of poetry.' It is true that a great deal of Dame Edith's early work does consist of technical exercises, some delightfully successful, others mere patterns of sound independent of meaning. Yet these exercises were essential to her development, for by their means she was perfecting a highly individual technique. One of her main preoccupations was with texture (which she considered to be akin to tone in music) and 'the effect of texture upon rhythm and upon speed of poetry', which necessitated a prolonged study of assonance and dissonance, and of the sound values of vowels and consonants. Many of the poems in her early books—*Clowns Houses* (1918), *The Wooden Pegasus* (1920), *Bucolic Comedies* (1923) and *Façade* (1926)—were, therefore, in the nature of technical explorations of the musical potentialities of words and phrases in various contexts.

Another of Dame Edith's special characteristics was her practice of sense transfusion—that is, the description of impressions received by one sense in terms usually confined to another, or at its most complex, the presentation of two or more sense impressions in a single concentrated phrase. Thus, when she was successful she was able to convey the unity of total experience, for sense impressions are seldom completely isolated one from another. The influence of Rimbaud, who anticipated her in this field of experiment, can be seen in her early poems in the preoccupation with the enchanting but private world of her own childhood, with its peculiar mental climate and atmosphere, its stage props and its landscapes inhabited by imaginary and fairylike characters—kings, queens and princesses, goose-girls and kitchen maids, negroes and witches, good and bad fairies, together with odd creations of her own, such as black Mrs Behemoth, Sir Pompey Alexander and Colonel Fantock. Her habit of repeating certain themes, symbolic figures and phrases in different poems not only connected the separate pieces, despite the variants in treatment, but carried the cumulative emotional force from one poem to the next. Many of these echoes and repetitions, however, were hardly significant enough to justify the process so that, instead of enriching the new context by recalling the previous poetic experience, they served merely to weaken the impact of what was being communicated.

To many of the critics of the twenties, it appeared as if, unattuned to the conditions of her age, Edith Sitwell was deliberately turning her back on modern life and seeking a refuge in the memories of childhood, and some of the autobiographical fragments embedded in her poetry seemed to lend support to this view. Nevertheless, it can now be seen that the work which followed and which has been so widely acclaimed was, in fact, the natural outcome of early experiments. 'Pedagogues', the concluding stanzas of 'Elegy for Dead Fashion', parts of 'The Sleeping Beauty', and a few isolated themes from *Façade* can certainly be identified with the later pieces; but it is in her technique rather than choice of subject that the poet's development can most clearly be distinguished. With the publication of *Gold Coast Customs* (1929), Dame Edith showed that, if until then she had confined her attention to a detailed exploration of the dream world of her own lost childhood, she was as deeply concerned with the social evils of her generation as any of her contemporaries; and in this long poem she attempted to come to grips with them.

For over ten years after *Gold Coast Customs*, Dame Edith wrote little or no poetry, but with the outbreak of the second world war she seemed to acquire a fresh burst of creative energy and a new sense of urgency became apparent in her work. The poem, 'Still Falls the Rain', written in 1940, and included in the volume entitled *Street Songs* (1942) marks the turning point:

> Still falls the Rain—
> Dark as the world of man, black as our loss—

Blind as the nineteen hundred and forty nails
Upon the cross.

The poem is concerned with the human predicament, the selfish
and destructive powers of man, and the evil generated by man
himself—in a world which can be redeemed by the love of God,
as revealed in Christ.

Street Songs, followed by *Green Song* (1944), *The Song of the
Cold* (1945), *The Shadow of Cain* (1947) and *The Canticle of the
Rose* (1949), contain the finest poems Dame Edith wrote during a
lifetime devoted to poetry.

During the last fifty years or so the poets who have attracted
most public attention have been those whose individual talents
and awareness of the age have compelled them to forge new styles
of expression (Yeats, Eliot, Auden and Dylan Thomas) or, among
the less gifted, those who have been quick to appreciate and exploit
the prevalent fashions. If this has had a revitalising effect on the
rhythms and language of poetry, it has also been responsible
for the neglect of some fine poets who have been content to
pursue their own lines of development within the main stream of
tradition.

EDWIN MUIR is one of the most important of these poets, and
it is highly probable that, as his poetry becomes better known and
understood, his reputation will steadily be enhanced. When we
remember that during the whole period of his poetic career the
reading public has been loud in its condemnation of the 'obscurity'
of modern poetry, it seems odd that Muir has not been selected
for official approval and held up as an example. The truth is, of
course, that despite the apparent simplicity of his work and his
use of traditional forms, Muir's poetry—like all good poetry—
demands an effort on the part of the reader. Moreover, Muir was
always, to some extent, isolated as a poet and deliberately re-
mained outside the temporary influences of literary movements
and fashionable trends. He avoided the limelight. To say that
Muir was a traditionalist, however, is not to imply that his work
was not original, nor that he was unaware of the problems of his
age; for, as is shown by the poems he wrote during the forties, he

achieved a maturity of thought rare among poets of this century and was acutely conscious of the human condition.

As a result of the circumstances of his life, Muir did not start writing poetry until he was thirty-five and it took him a considerable time to come to terms, both with himself and with his earlier experience. In his *Autobiography* he tells us that when he adopted Christianity somewhat late in his career, he suddenly became aware that he had in fact been a Christian for many years without realising it. His themes were the same throughout his life—the conflict between good and evil, between time and eternity, between innocence and guilt—but perhaps his most characteristic subject was that of man's spiritual quest, which he explored from every aspect in poem after poem—'Hölderlin's Journey', 'The Stationary Journey', 'The Road', 'The Voyage', 'The Labyrinth' etc.—making extensive use of Jungian psychology and Greek and Christian myth in the process. His work as a literary journalist and as the translator of Kafka and other European writers during the twenties and thirties, combined with his own experiences in Europe, may have added a European outlook to his other qualities; certainly they gave him fresh insight into European problems. Reviewing one of his books, Dom Moraes observed: 'A poem like "The Interrogation" might have been written by a Polish Jew. . . . I mean that in the curious sense they express of immediate evil threatening possible good they have a dimension and depth beyond what other English poets writing at the time . . . ever achieved.'

Like Edith Sitwell, Muir did not attain either the mastery of his craft or the understanding necessary to his maturity as a major poet until the forties. It was as if the war and the years immediately following enabled him to crystallise his ideas and embody what he had learned from his experience of life in a language of new fluency and power. The poems included in *The Labyrinth* represent the peak of his achievement.

VERNON WATKINS was born in Wales and, apart from a short spell at Cambridge, spent practically the whole of his life there; it is therefore tragically ironic that he should die on a visit to the United States in 1967. Although his poetry can most fittingly be described as religious and metaphysical, it derives its power from the natural world and can at time be as elementally simple as the sea which breaks upon the rocky coast of Wales and which is always present, if only as an undertone, in his work. The regional element in his poetry can be discerned in his landscapes and seascapes, and in his use of Welsh legend and folklore and symbols drawn from childhood memories. For instance, his first book of poems, *The Ballad of the Mari Lwyd* (1941), took its title from a long poem based on a folk custom which the poet remembered from childhood. In certain parts of Wales it was still the custom, on the last night of the year, for a carved horse's head, or a horse's skull, decorated with ribands, to be carried from house to house by a party of singers, who tried to win admission to food and drink in a rhyming contest with those inside the house. 'I have attempted,' wrote Watkins in a note to the poem, 'to bring together those who are separated. The last breath of the year is their threshold, the moment of supreme forgiveness, confusion and understanding, the profane and sacred moment impossible to realise while the clock hands divide the Living and the Dead.'

'The Collier', in the same volume, shows that Watkins felt sympathy for the people of the Welsh mining community, but even here the protagonist is identified with the archetypal Joseph of the Old Testament. Watkins's early poetry suffers from the undue influence of Yeats and a tendency towards Celtic exuberance, resulting occasionally in mere sound and fury (see his *The Lamp and the Veil*, 1945), but as he developed his style he acquired a superb mastery over language, without losing his incantatory power.

His third book, *The Lady with the Unicorn* (1948), reveals that, without losing the human touch and his concern for individuals, Watkins had at last succeeded in incorporating the whole body of mythology into a creative pattern within the framework of which his philosophy, symbols and intricate verbal tapestries have their profoundest effect; a pattern which is inevitably Christian in its presentation of values, and comprehensive enough to lend itself to the felicities of art and nature.

In the prefatory note to his *Collected Poems* (1952), DYLAN THOMAS said: 'These poems, with all their crudities, doubts, and confusions, are written for the love of Man and in praise of

God, and I'd be a damn' fool if they weren't.' Yet many critics still refuse to take him at his word and insist on describing his poetry as 'pantheistic'. From the time that his work began to appear, Thomas was preoccupied with spiritual values and the ultimates of existence, related through his peculiar, and in some ways almost mystical, vision of sex, which he regarded as the unifying force of all creation. Despite the legends of his outrageously bohemian mode of life, and the circumstances surrounding his death, Dylan Thomas was a naturally religious poet. With the Welsh Bethel as its probable source, his religious faith was so firmly implanted and so much a part of his poetic make-up that he was never at pains to declare it; or to attempt to define his beliefs in relation to experience. God, for him, was an established fact, and divine manifestations were to be celebrated rather than examined or questioned. It is true that in his earliest poetry the religious element was obscured because he was so engrossed in sexual and prenatal experience. Though his early poems were rich in Biblical symbols and allusions, it was simply in order to express his own sexual interpretation of life and death.

Of the poems in Thomas's second collection, *Twenty-Five Poems* (1936), the poem entitled 'And death shall have no dominion' is one of the most significant to any study of his development—first, because it marks a definite change in Thomas's attitude towards death; secondly, because it envisages human love as a dynamic force without limiting it to its sexual elements as do most of the earlier poems; and finally because it celebrates what may reasonably be termed a Christian conception of life, death and resurrection, if not entirely an orthodox one in all its implications. Taking the poem as a whole, one can say that in this poem for the first time the unity of life is recognised by the poet to be of a spiritual rather than a physical order. Since the text of Romans 6 in the Bible is the starting-point of the poem, and the passage from which the theme is derived, it is important to the understanding of the poem: *Now if we be dead with Christ, we believe that we shall also live with him; Knowing that Christ being raised from the dead dieth no more; Death hath no more dominion over him.* In the light of this passage it will be seen that the poem is neither an expression of some vaguely held belief in an after-life nor a 'further example of the poet's pantheism'.

Such lines as

> Though they go mad they shall be sane

and

> Twisting on racks when sinews give way,
> Strapped to a wheel, yet they shall not break . . .

would surely have little significance in these days of brainwashing and prison camps if all they were intended to mean was that at death man would merely achieve an impersonal state of oneness with nature.

In his third book, *The Map of Love* (1939), the poet acknowledges his state of conflict and admits that 'it is the sinner's dust-tongued bell claps me to churches', but, with one important exception, the poems in this collection are of a transitional character. The exception is 'After the Funeral', subtitled 'In Memory of Ann Jones'. Previously, his poems dealing with birth and death, his favourite subjects, were strictly impersonalised. They were concerned with man on his journey from womb to grave and failed to communicate any feeling for anyone in particular. In 'After the Funeral' we find out only that the new attitude to death and to human love is more positively presented, but that Thomas is concerned with a particular individual, the old aunt with whom he often stayed as a child, and all his natural affection, combined with respect and humility, is communicated to the reader.

It seems to me that 'After the Funeral', with its intensely human sympathy, continues the line of development from 'And death shall have no dominion' to the magnificent elegy, 'A Refusal to Mourn the Death, By Fire, of a Child in London' in his last separate book of poems, *Deaths and Entrances* (1946). If *Deaths and Entrances* can hardly be said to reveal a new Thomas, since many of the features which make it so successful can be traced to his earlier work, it does show a new integrating force was in operation, as if something which had previously been suppressed had suddenly thrust itself forth into the light and taken control. Certainly such poems as 'This Side of Truth', 'The Conversation of Prayer', 'Holy Spring' and 'There Was a Saviour' provide evidence of a complete change of outlook, and the most sceptical reader could not miss the Christian exultation of 'Vision and Prayer', so reminiscent of Herbert in its hourglass form and of Thompson's 'Hound of Heaven' in its mysticism.

Thomas's antipathy towards dogma of any kind makes it extremely difficult to ascertain the real nature of the religious convictions he held towards the end of his life, or to identify them with orthodox Christian beliefs at more than a few isolated points. Even when he appeared to be on the verge of committing himself there were inconsistencies and contradictions which cannot be attributed to poetic licence; for in his later poems, Thomas paid more attention to craftsmanship than ever before. There is, however, no ambiguity about the conclusion to 'Poem on his Birthday', one of the last poems he wrote, in which he counts his blessings:

> And this last blessing most,
>
> That the closer I move
> To death, one man through his sundered hulks,
> The louder the sun blooms
> And the tusked, ramshackling sea exults,
> And every wave of the way
> And gale I tackle, the whole world then,
> With more triumphant faith
> Than ever was since the world was said,
> Spins its morning of praise. . . .
>
> . . . . As I sail out to die.

Whatever else the discerning reader may find in the poetry of NORMAN NICHOLSON, he can hardly fail to notice the two major elements which go to its creation: the poet's wholehearted acceptance of Christianity as a pattern for living, and the intensity of his feelings for the Cumbrian landscape, people and way of life.

Nicholson is an Anglican by choice, but as a child he was thrown into close contact with Celtic evangelistic Methodism (via the Cornish miners), which made a lasting impression on his mind. 'If I have any power of rhetoric,' he remarked in a letter to the editor of this volume, 'I believe it derives from the old Methodist preachers.' His early work was packed with Christian images and terminology, and he frequently drew on biblical episodes for his subjects, though his approach was always highly original and his diction sufficiently novel to rouse and maintain the interest even of those who did not accept his beliefs, except when he overstepped the bounds of congruity with such phrases as—'preserved in gelatine of Jesus' blood'. In his longer and more specifically religious poems he attempted to deal with traditional themes from a new angle, but if the way in which he developed his ideas and controlled his material commanded respect, the result was not entirely successful. The religious element in his work was more convincingly expressed in less ambitious poems like 'Rockferns':

> Why need I fear the bursting bomb
> Or whatsoever death should come,
> If brains and bowels be cast forth
> Splintered to spleenwort on the earth?
> And if a subtler part may cruise
> Twice round the sun and Betelgeuse,
> My soul shall detonate on high
> And plant itself in cracks of sky.

Rock Face (1948), his second volume of poems, signalised an important phase in Nicholson's development. With the publication of this volume it became evident that he was paying far less attention to the superficial aspects of Christianity and more to its intrinsic values. The few scriptural images to be found were confined to descriptive phrases—'Chimneys are Lot's wives of salt'—and poems appropriate to the occasion ('Caedmon'). The material was more assimilated, too. In 'To a Child Before Birth', for instance, he emphasises the individual's need to attain some measure of independence in order to reach moral and spiritual maturity. Paradoxically, he chooses the frailest of individuals to make his point, the unborn child.

It is, however, Nicholson's regional outlook and feeling which make him so indubitably a poet of the universal. His poems flow so spontaneously that the Cumberland landscape of fells and tarns, of the hills and the sea, and even 'the chimneys, pitshafts, rubbletips' of the mining areas, are everywhere apparent. In the earlier poems the introduction of place-names like Wrynose,

Walna Scar and Wallabarrow Crag, local traditions and person-alities, added a native texture to his work, and his vigorous lang-uage marked him out as a poet of considerable talent. Many of his poems were purely descriptive, but however simple the theme, the keenness of his eye and ear never allowed him to lapse into occasional verse. He proved himself to be a master in the elements of surprise, and because he combined a sensitive perception with a delightful and almost daring use of image and metaphor, he was able to tackle subjects which most of his contemporaries avoided.

With the publication of *Rock Face* it became clear that there had been a further development in the regional aspect of his work, too. For some years Nicholson had been inclined to exclude Millom, the small industrial town in which he lived, from his consideration because, with its slagbanks, ironworks, iron ore mines, and dismal sprawl, it seemed so alien to the countryside surrounding it. Then he gradually began to recognise that the town was just as much a part of the landscape as the fells and lakes; they belonged to each other. As the poet himself observed in a broadcast: 'I did not need to go out into the hills to see what the Lake District rocks looked like. My own home is roofed over with slates of Kirkby Moor . . . and there are slabs of stone laid as a paving to the yard. . . . So, in my eyes, Millom was gradually reabsorbed into the landscape, becoming one with the rock, the soil, the seasons and the weather.'

Perhaps the most striking feature of this new development is Nicholson's preoccupation with the creative and cyclic processes of life, expressed mainly in terms of landscape and geology (see 'Silecroft Shore'). It is this long-range vision of the continuity and purpose of life manifest in his approach to the simplest of themes which unifies much of his poetry and distinguishes it from that of his contemporaries. As a result, his work not only shows greater depths of thought and imagination, but it is more authentic in expressing the Christian interpretation of life in terms of his own experience and environment.

Edith Sitwell

from STREET SONGS 1942

Still Falls the Rain

The Raids, 1940.   *Night and Dawn*

Still falls the Rain—
Dark as the world of man, black as our loss—
Blind as the nineteen hundred and forty nails
Upon the Cross.

Still falls the Rain
With a sound like the pulse of the heart that is changed
    to the hammer-beat
In the Potter's Field, and the sound of the impious feet

On the Tomb:
              Still falls the Rain
In the Field of Blood where the small hopes breed and
    the human brain
Nurtures its greed, that worm with the brow of Cain.

Still falls the Rain
At the feet of the Starved Man hung upon the Cross.
Christ that each day, each night, nails there, have mercy
    on us—
On Dives and on Lazarus:
Under the Rain the sore and the gold are as one.

Still falls the Rain—
Still falls the Blood from the Starved Man's wounded
    Side:

He bears in His Heart all wounds,—those of the light
      that died,
The last faint spark
In the self-murdered heart, the wounds of the sad
      uncomprehending dark,
The wounds of the baited bear,—
The blind and weeping bear whom the keepers beat
On his helpless flesh . . . the tears of the hunted hare.

Still falls the Rain—
Then—O Ile leape up to my God: who pulles me doune—
See, see where Christ's blood streames in the firmament:
It flows from the Brow we nailed upon the tree
Deep to the dying, to the thirsting heart
That holds the fires of the world,—dark-smirched with
      pain
As Caesar's laurel crown.

Then sounds the voice of One who like the heart of man
Was once a child who among beasts has lain—
'Still do I love, still shed my innocent light, my Blood,
      for thee.'

Lullaby

Though the world has slipped and gone,
Sounds my loud discordant cry
Like the steel birds' song on high:
'Still one thing is left—the Bone!'
Then out danced the Babioun.

She sat in the hollow of the sea—
A socket whence the eye's put out—
She sang to the child a lullaby
(The steel birds' nest was thereabout).

'Do, do, do, do—
Thy mother's hied to the vaster race:
The Pterodactyl made its nest
And laid a steel egg in her breast—
Under the Judas-coloured sun.
She'll work no more, nor dance, nor moan,
And I am come to take her place.
Do, do.

There's nothing left but earth's low bed—
(The Pterodactyl fouls its nest):
But steel wings fan thee to thy rest,
And wingless truth and larvae lie
And eyeless hope and handless fear—
All these for thee as toys are spread,
Do—do—

Red is the bed of Poland, Spain,
And thy mother's breast, who has grown wise
In that fouled nest. If she could rise,
Give birth again,

In wolfish pelt she'd hide thy bones
To shield thee from the world's long cold,
And down on all fours shouldst thou crawl
For thus from no height canst thou fall—
Do, do.

She'd give no hands: there's naught to hold
And naught to make: there's dust to sift,
But no food for the hands to lift.
Do, do.

Heed my ragged lullaby,
Fear not living, fear not chance;
All is equal—blindness, sight,
There is no depth, there is no height:
Do, do.

The Judas-coloured sun is gone,
And with the Ape thou art alone—
Do,
　　Do.'

Serenade: Any Man to Any Woman

Dark angel who art clear and straight
As cannon shining in the air,
Your blackness doth invade my mind
And thunderous as the armoured wind
That rained on Europe is your hair;

And so I love you till I die—
(Unfaithful I, the cannon's mate):
Forgive my love of such brief span,
But fickle is the flesh of man,
And death's cold puts the passion out.

I'll woo you with a serenade—
The wolfish howls the starving made;
And lies shall be your canopy
To shield you from the freezing sky.

Yet when I clasp you in my arms—
Who are my sleep, the zero hour
That clothes, instead of flesh, my heart,—
You in my heaven have no part,
For you, my mirage broken in flower,

Can never see what dead men know!
Then die with me and be my love:
The grave shall be your shady grove
And in your pleasaunce rivers flow

(To ripen this new Paradise)
From a more universal Flood
Than Noah knew: but yours is blood.

Yet still you will imperfect be
That in my heart like death's chill grows,
—A rainbow shining in the night,
30   Born of my tears . . . your lips, the bright
Summer-old folly of the rose.

from GREEN SONG 1944

A Mother to her Dead Child

The winter, the animal sleep of the earth is over
And in the warmth of the affirming sun
All beings, beasts, men, planets, waters, move
Freed from the imprisoning frost, acclaim their love
That is the light of the sun.
                    So the first spring began
Within the heart before the Fall of Man.

The earth puts forth its sprays, the heart its warmth,
And your hands push back the dark that is your nurse,
Feel for my heart as in the days before your birth.
10   O Sun of my life, return to the waiting earth
Of your mother's breast, the heart, the empty arms.
Come soon, for the time is passing, and when I am old
The night of my body will be too thick and cold
For the sun of your growing heart. Return from your new
        mother
The earth: she is too old for your little body,
Too old for the small tendernesses, the kissings
In the soft tendrils of your hair. The earth is so old
She can only think of darkness and sleep, forgetting
That children are restless like the small spring shadows.
20   But the huge pangs of winter and the pain
Of the spring's birth, the endless centuries of rain
Will not lay bare your trusting smile, your tress,
Or lay your heart bare to my heart again
In your small earthly dress.

84

And when I wait for you upon the summer roads
They bear all things and men, business and pleasure,
    sorrow,
And lovers' meetings, mourning shades, the poor man's
    leisure,
And the foolish rose that cares not ever for the far
    tomorrow,
But the roads are too busy for the sound of your feet,
And the lost men, the rejected of life, who tend the wounds
That life has made as if they were a new sunrise, whose
    human speech is dying
From want, to the rusted voice of the tiger, turn not
    their heads lest I hear your child-voice crying
In that hoarse tiger-voice: 'I am hungry! am cold!'
Lest I see your smile upon lips that were made for the
    kiss that exists not,
The food that deserts them,—those lips never warm with
    love, but from the world's fever,
Whose smile is a gap into darkness, the breaking apart
Of the long-impending earthquake that waits in the heart.
That smile rends the soul with the sign of its destitution,
It drips from the last long pangs of the heart, self-
    devouring,
And tearing the seer.

                 Yet one will return to the lost men,
Whose heart is the Sun of Reason, dispelling the shadow
That was born with no eyes to shed tears,—bringing
    peace to the lust
And pruriency of the Ape, from the human heart's
    sublimity
And tenderness teaching the dust that it is holy,
And to those who are hungry, are naked and cold as the
    worm, who are bare as the spirit
In that last night when the rich and the poor are alone,
Bringing love like the daily bread, like the light at
    morning.
And knowing this, I would give you again, my day's
    darling,
My little child who preferred the bright apple to gold,

And who lies with the shining world on his innocent
      eyes,
Though night-long I feel your tears, bright as the rose
In its sorrowful leaves, on my lips, and feel your hands
Touching my cheek, and wondering 'Are those your tears?'
O grief, that your heart should know the tears that seem
      empty years
And the worlds that are falling!

Heart and Mind

Said the Lion to the Lioness—'When you are amber
      dust,—
No more a raging fire like the heat of the Sun
(No liking but all lust)—
Remember still the flowering of the amber blood and bone
The rippling of bright muscles like a sea,
Remember the rose-prickles of bright paws
Though we shall mate no more
Till the fire of that sun the heart and the moon-cold
      bone are one.'

Said the Skeleton lying upon the sands of Time—
10 'The great gold planet that is the mourning heat of the
      Sun
Is greater than all gold, more powerful
Than the tawny body of a Lion that fire consumes
Like all that grows or leaps . . . so is the heart
More powerful than all dust. Once I was Hercules
Or Samson, strong as the pillars of the seas:
But the flames of the heart consumed me, and the mind
Is but a foolish wind.'

Said the Sun to the Moon—'When you are but a lonely
      white crone,
And I, a dead King in my golden armour somewhere in
      a dark wood,

Remember only this of our hopeless love
That never till Time is done
Will the fire of the heart and the fire of the mind be one.'

from THE CANTICLE OF THE ROSE 1949

THREE POEMS OF THE ATOMIC BOMB

1. Dirge for the New Sunrise

*(Fifteen minutes past eight o'clock, on the morning of Monday
the 6th of August 1945)*

Bound to my heart as Ixion to the wheel,
Nailed to my heart as the Thief upon the Cross,
I hang between our Christ and the gap where the world was
        lost

And watch the phantom Sun in Famine Street
—The ghost of the heart of Man . . . red Cain
And the more murderous brain
Of Man, still redder Nero that conceived the death
Of his mother Earth, and tore
Her womb, to know the place where he was conceived.

But no eyes grieved—
For none were left for tears:
They were blinded as the years
Since Christ was born. Mother or Murderer, you have
        given or taken life—
Now all is one!

There was a morning when the holy Light
Was young. The beautiful First Creature came
To our water-springs, and thought us without blame.

Our hearts seemed safe in our breasts and sang to the
        Light—
The marrow in the bone
20   We dreamed was safe . . . the blood in the veins, the sap
        in the tree
Were springs of Deity.

But I saw the little Ant-men as they ran
Carrying the world's weight of the world's filth
And the filth in the heart of Man—
Compressed till those lusts and greeds had a greater heat
        than that of the Sun.

And the ray from that heat came soundless, shook the sky
As if in search of food, and squeezed the stems
Of all that grows on the earth till they were dry
—And drank the marrow of the bone:
30   The eyes that saw, the lips that kissed, are gone
Or black as thunder lie and grin at the murdered Sun.

The living blind and seeing Dead together lie
As if in love. . . . There was no more hating then,
And no more love: Gone is the heart of Man.

2. The Shadow of Cain

(*To C. M. Bowra*)

Under great yellow flags and banners of the ancient Cold
Began the huge migrations
From some primeval disaster in the heart of Man.

There were great oscillations
Of temperature. . . . You knew there had once been warmth;

But the Cold is the highest mathematical Idea . . . the Cold
        is Zero—
The Nothing from which arose

All Being and all variation. . . . It is the sound too high
        for our hearing, the Point that flows
Till it becomes the line of Time . . . an endless positing
Of Nothing, or the Ideal that tries to burgeon
Into Reality through multiplying. Then Time froze

To immobility and changed to Space.
Black flags among the ice, blue rays
And the purple perfumes of the polar Sun
Freezing the bone to sapphire and to zircon—
These were our days.

And now in memory of great oscillations
Of temperature in that epoch of the Cold,
We found a continent of turquoise, vast as Asia
In the yellowing airs of the Cold: the tooth of a mammoth;
And there, in a gulf, a dark pine-sword

To show there had once been warmth and the gulf stream
        in our veins
Where only the Chaos of the Antarctic Pole
Or the peace of its atonic coldness reigns.

And sometimes we found the trace
Of a bird's claw in the immensity of the Cold:
The trace of the first letters we could not read:
Some message of Man's need,

And of the slow subsidence of a Race;
And of great heats in which the Pampean mud was formed,
In which the Megatherium Mylodon
Lies buried under Mastodon-trumpetings of leprous Suns.

The Earth had cloven in two in that primal disaster.
But when the glacial period began
There was still some method of communication
Between Man and his brother Man—
Although their speech
Was alien, each from each
As the Bird's from the Tiger's, born from the needs of our
        opposing famines.

40 Each said 'This is the Race of the Dead . . . their blood
        is cold . . .
    For the heat of those more recent on the Earth
    Is higher . . . the blood-beat of the Bird more high
    Than that of the ancient race of the primeval Tiger':
    The Earth had lived without the Bird

    In that Spring when there were no flowers like thunders
        in the air.
    And now Earth lies flat beneath the shade of an iron wing.
    And of what does the Pterodactyl sing—
    Of what red buds in what tremendous Spring?'

    The thunders of the Spring began. . . . We came again
50 After that long migration
    To the city built before the Flood by our brother Cain.

    And when we reached an open door
    The Fate said 'My feet ache.'
    The Wanderers said 'Our hearts ache.'

    There was great lightning
    In flashes coming to us over the floor:
    The Whiteness of the Bread
    The Whiteness of the Dead
    The Whiteness of the Claw—
60 All this coming to us in flashes through the open door.

    There were great emerald thunders in the air
    In the violent Spring, the thunders of the sap and the blood
        in the heart
    —The Spiritual Light, the physical Revelation.
    In the streets of the City of Cain there were great Rainbows
    Of Emeralds: the young people, crossing and meeting.

    And everywhere
    The great voice of the Sun in sap and bud
    Fed from the heart of Being, the panic Power,

The sacred Fury, shouts of Eternity
To the blind eyes, the heat in the wingèd seed, the fire
in the blood.

And through the works of Death,
The dust's aridity, is heard the sound
Of mounting saps like monstrous bull-voices of unseen
fearful mimes:
And the great rolling world-wide thunders of that drumming
underground

Proclaim our Christ, and roar 'Let there be harvest!
Let there be no more Poor—
For the Son of God is sowed in every furrow!'

We did not heed the Cloud in the Heavens shaped like
the hand
Of Man. . . . But there came a roar as if the Sun and
Earth had come together—
The Sun descending and the Earth ascending
To take its place above . . . the Primal Matter
Was broken, the womb from which all life began.
Then to the murdered Sun a totem pole of dust arose in
memory of Man.

The cataclysm of the Sun down-pouring
Seemed the roar
Of those vermilion Suns the drops of the blood
That bellowing like Mastodons at war
Rush down the length of the world—away—away—

The violence of torrents, cataracts, maelstroms, rains
That went before the Flood—
These covered the earth from the freshets of our brothers'
veins;

And with them, the forked lightnings of the gold
From the split mountains,
Blasting their rivals, the young foolish wheat-ears
Amid those terrible rains.

91

The gulf that was torn across the world seemed as if the
        beds of all the Oceans
Were emptied. . . . Naked, and gaping at what once had
        been the Sun,
Like the mouth of the Universal Famine
It stretched its jaws from one end of the Earth to the other.

100 And in that hollow lay the body of our brother
Lazarus, upheaved from the world's tomb.
He lay in that great Death like the gold in the husk
Of the world . . . and round him, like spent lightnings, lay
        the Ore—
The balm for the world's sore.

And the gold lay in its husk of rough earth like the core
In the furred almond, the chestnut in its prickly
Bark, the walnut in a husk green and bitter.

And to that hollow sea
The Civilisation of the Maimed, and, too, Life's lepers,
        came
110 As once to Christ near the Sea of Galilee.

They brought the Aeons of Blindness and the Night
Of the World, crying to him, 'Lazarus, give us sight!
O you whose sores are of gold, who are the new Light
Of the World!'
                They brought to the Tomb
The Condemned of Man, who wear as stigmata from the
        womb
The depression of the skull as in the lesser
Beasts of Prey, the marks of Ape and Dog,

The canine and lemurine muscle . . . the pitiable, the
        terrible,
120 The loveless, whose deformities arose
Before their birth, or from a betrayal by the gold wheat-ear.
'Lazarus, for all love we knew the great Sun's kiss

On the loveless cheek. He came to the dog-fang and the
    lion-claw
That Famine gave the empty mouth, the workless hands.
He came to the inner leaf of the forsaken heart—
He spoke of our Christ, and of a golden love. . . .
But our Sun is gone . . . will your gold bring warmth to
    the loveless lips, and harvest to barren lands?'

Then Dives was brought. . . . He lay like a leprous Sun
That is covered with the sores of the world . . . the leprosy
Of gold encrusts the world that was his heart.

Like a great ear of wheat that is swoln with grain,
Then ruined by white rain,
He lay. . . . His hollow face, dust white, was cowled with
    a hood of gold:
But you saw there was no beat or pulse of blood—
You would not know him now from Lazarus!

He did not look at us.
He said 'What was spilt still surges like the Flood.
But Gold shall be the Blood
Of the world. . . . Brute gold condemned to the primal
    essence
Has the texture, smell, warmth, colour of Blood. We must
    take

A quintessence of the disease for remedy. Once hold
The primal matter of all gold—
From which it grows
(That Rose of the World) as the sharp clear tree from the
    seed of the great rose,

Then give of this, condensed to the transparency
Of the beryl, the weight of twenty barley grains:
And the leper's face will be full as the rose's face
After great rains.

It will shape again the Shadow of Man. Or at least will take
150 From all roots of life the symptoms of the leper—
And make the body sharp as the honeycomb,
The roots of life that are left like the red roots of the
      rose-branches.'

But near him a gold sound—
The voice of an unborn wheat-ear accusing Dives,
Said 'Soon I shall be more rare, more precious than gold.'

There are no thunders, there are no fires, no suns, no
      earthquakes
Left in our blood. . . . But yet like the rolling thunders of
      all the fires in the world, we cry
To Dives: 'You are the shadow of Cain. Your shade is the
      primal Hunger.'
'I lie under what condemnation?'
160 The same as Adam, the same as Cain, the same as Sodom,
the same as Judas.

And the fires of your Hell shall not be quenched by the
      rain
From those torn and parti-coloured garments of Christ,
      those rags
That once were Men. Each wound, each stripe,
Cries out more loudly than the voice of Cain—
Saying "Am I my brother's keeper?"' Think! When the last
      clamour of the Bought and Sold
The agony of Gold
Is hushed. . . . When the last Judas-kiss
Has died upon the cheek of the Starved Man Christ, those
      ashes that were men
Will rise again
170 To be our Fires upon the Judgment Day!
And yet—who dreamed that Christ has died in vain?
He walks again on the Seas of Blood, He comes in the
      terrible Rain.

3. The Canticle of the Rose

(To Geoffrey Gorer)

The Rose upon the wall
Cries—'I am the voice of Fire:
And in me grows
The pomegranate splendour of Death, the ruby, garnet,
almandine
Dews: Christ's Wounds in me shine.

I rise upon my stem,
The Flower, the whole Plant-being, produced by Light
With all Plant-systems and formations.... As in Fire
All elements dissolve, so in one bright
10   Ineffable essence all Plant-being dissolves to make the
Flower.

My stem rises bright:
Organic water polarised to the dark
Earth-centre, and to Light.'

Below that wall, in Famine Street
There is nothing left but the heart to eat

And the Shade of Men.... Buyers and sellers cry
'Speak not the name of Light—
Her name is Madness now.... Though we are black
beneath her kiss
As if she were the Sun, her name is Night:
20   She has condemned us, and decreed that Man must die.'

There was a woman combing her long hair
To the rhythm of the river flowing....
She sang 'All things will end—
Like the sound of Time in my veins growing:
The hump on the dwarf, the mountain on the plain,
The fixed red of the rose and the rainbow's red,
The fires of the heart, the wandering planet's pain—
All loss, all gain—
Yet will the world remain!'

30 The song died in the Ray. . . . Where is she now?
Dissolved, and gone—
And only her red shadow stains the unremembering stone.

And in Famine Street the sellers cry
'What will you buy?

A dress for the Bride?'
(But all the moulds of generation died
Beneath that Ray.)
                              'Or a winding-sheet?'
(Outworn. . . . The Dead have nothing left to hide.)

40 'Then buy' said the Fate arisen from Hell—
That thing of rags and patches—
'A box of matches!
For the machine that generated warmth
Beneath your breast is dead. . . . You need a fire
To warm what lies upon your bone. . . .
Not all the ashes of your brother Men
Will kindle that again—
Nor all the world's incendiaries!
Who buys—Who buys—?
50 Come, give me pence to lay upon my staring lidless
          eyes!'

But high upon the wall
The Rose where the Wounds of Christ are red
Cries to the Light
'See how I rise upon my stem, ineffable bright
Effluence of bright essence. . . . From my little span
I cry of Christ, Who is the ultimate Fire
Who will burn away the cold in the heart of Man. . . . '
Springs come, springs go. . . .
'I was reddere on Rode than the Rose in the rayne.'
60   'This smel is Crist, clepid the plantynge of the Rose in
          Jerico.'

Edwin Muir

from THE NARROW PLACE 1943

The Wayside Station

Here at the wayside station, as many a morning,
I watch the smoke torn from the fumy engine
Crawling across the field in serpent sorrow.
Flat in the east, held down by stolid clouds,
The struggling day is born and shines already
On its warm hearth far off. Yet something here
Glimmers along the ground to show the seagulls
White on the furrows' black unturning waves.

But now the light has broadened.
I watch the farmstead on the little hill,
That seems to mutter: 'Here is day again'
Unwillingly. Now the sad cattle wake
In every byre and stall,
The ploughboy stirs in the loft, the farmer groans
And feels the day like a familiar ache
Deep in his body, though the house is dark.
The lovers part

Now in the bedroom where the pillows gleam
Great and mysterious as deep hills of snow,
An inaccessible land. The wood stands waiting
While the bright snare slips coil by coil around it,
Dark silver on every branch. The lonely stream
That rode through darkness leaps the gap of light,
Its voice grown loud, and starts its winding journey
Through the day and time and war and history.

The Narrow Place

How all the roads creep in.
This place has grown so narrow,
You could not swing a javelin,
And if you shot an arrow,
It would skim this meagre mountain wall
And in some other country
Like a lost meteor fall.
When first this company
Took root here no one knows,
For nothing comes and goes
But the bleak mountain wind,
That so our blood has thinned
And sharpened so our faces—
Unanswerably grave
As long-forsaken places—
They have lost all look of hate or love
And keep but what they have.
The cloud has drawn so close,
This small much-trodden mound
Must, must be very high
And no road goes by.
The parsimonious ground
That at its best will bear
A few thin blades as fine as hair
Can anywhere be found,
Yet is so proud and niggardly
And envious, it will trust
Only one little wild half-leafless tree
To straggle from the dust.

Yet under it we sometimes feel such
        ease
As if it were ten thousand trees
And for its foliage had
Robbed half the world of shade.
All the woods in grief
Bowed down by leaf and bird and leaf

From all their branches could not weep
A sleep such as that sleep.

Sleep underneath the tree.
It is your murdering eyes that make
The sterile hill, the standing lake
And the leaf-breaking wind.
Then shut your eyes and see,
Sleep on and do not wake
Till there is movement in the lake,
And the club-headed water-serpents break
In emerald lightnings through the slime,
Making a mark on Time.

The Good Man in Hell

If a good man were ever housed in Hell
    By needful error of the qualities,
Perhaps to prove the rule or shame the devil,
    Or speak the truth only a stranger sees,

Would he, surrendering to obvious hate,
    Fill half eternity with cries and tears,
Or watch beside Hell's little wicket gate
    In patience for the first ten thousand years,

Feeling the curse climb slowly to his throat
    That, uttered, dooms him to rescindless ill,
Forcing his praying tongue to run by rote,
    Eternity entire before him still?

Would he at last, grown faithful in his station,
    Kindle a little hope in hopeles Hell,
And sow among the damned doubts of damnation,
    Since here someone could live and could live well?

One doubt of evil would bring down such a grace,
    Open such a gate, all Eden would enter in,
Hell be a place like any other place,
20   And love and hate and life and death begin.

from THE VOYAGE 1946

The Castle

All through that summer at ease we lay,
And daily from the turret wall
We watched the mowers in the hay
And the enemy half a mile away.
They seemed no threat to us at all.

For what, we thought, had we to fear
With our arms and provender, load on load,
Our towering battlements, tier on tier,
And friendly allies drawing near
10   On every leafy summer road.

Our gates were strong, our walls were thick,
So smooth and high, no man could win
A foothold there, no clever trick
Could take us, have us dead or quick.
Only a bird could have got in.

What could they offer us for bait?
Our captain was brave and we were true . . .
There was a little private gate,
A little wicked wicket gate.
20   The wizened warder let them through.

Oh then our maze of tunnelled stone
Grew thin and treacherous as air.
The cause was lost without a groan,
The famous citadel overthrown,
And all its secret galleries bare.

How can this shameful tale be told?
I will maintain until my death
We could do nothing, being sold;
Our only enemy was gold,
And we had no arms to fight it with.

Moses

He left us there, went up to Pisgah hill,
And saw the holiday land, the sabbath land,
The mild prophetic beasts, millenial herds,
The sacred lintel, over-arching tree,
The vineyards glittering on the southern slopes,
And in the midst the shining vein of water,
The river turning, turning towards its home.
Promised to us. The dream rose in his nostrils
With homely smell of wine and corn and cattle,
Byre, barn and stall, sweat-sanctified smell of peace.
He saw the tribes arrayed beside the river,
White robes and sabbath stillness, still light falling
On dark heads whitened by the desert wave,
The Sabbath of Sabbaths come and Canaan their home.
All this he saw in dreaming. But we who dream
Such common dreams and see so little saw
The battle for the land, the massacres,
The vineyards drenched in aboriginal blood,
The settlement, unsatisfactory order,
The petty wars and neighbouring jealousies
And local troubles. But we did not see,
We did not see and Moses did not see,
The great disaster, exile, diaspora,
The holy bread of the land crumbled and broken
In Babylon, Caesarea, Alexandria
As on a splendid dish, or gnawed as offal.
Nor did we see, beyond, the ghetto rising,
Toledo, Cracow, Vienna, Budapesth,

Nor, had we seen, would we have known our people
In the wild disguises of fantastic time,
Packed in dense cities, wandering countless roads,
And not a road in the world to lead them home.
How could we have seen such things? How could we have
    seen
That plot of ground pledged by the God of Moses
Trampled by sequent tribes, seized and forgotten
As a child seizes and forgets a toy,
Strange languages, strange gods and customs borne
Over it and away with the light migrations,
Stirring each century ancestral dust.

All this was settled while we stood by Jordan
That first great day, could not be otherwise.
Moses saw that day only; we did not see it;
But now it stands becalmed in time for ever:
White robes and sabbath peace, the snow-white emblem.'

from THE LABYRINTH 1949

The Labyrinth

Since I emerged that day from the labyrinth,
Dazed with the tall and echoing passages,
The swift recoils, so many I almost feared
I'd meet myself returning at some smooth corner,
Myself or my ghost, for all there was unreal
After the straw ceased rustling and the bull
Lay dead upon the straw and I remained,
Blood-splashed, if dead or alive I could not tell
In the twilight nothingness (I might have been
A spirit seeking his body through the roads
Of intricate Hades)—ever since I came out
To the world, the still fields swift with flowers, the
    trees

All bright with blossom, the little green hills, the
        sea,
The sky and all in movement under it,
Shepherds and flocks and birds and the young and old,
(I stared in wonder at the young and the old,
For in the maze time had not been with me;
I had strayed, it seemed, past sun and season and
        change,
Past rest and motion, for I could not tell
At last if I moved or strayed; the maze itself
Revolved around me on its hidden axis
And swept me smoothly to its enemy,
The lovely world)—since I came out that day,
There have been times when I have heard my footsteps
Still echoing in the maze, and all the roads
That run through the noisy world, deceiving streets
That meet and part and meet, and rooms that open
Into each other—and never a final room—
Stairways and corridors and antechambers
That vacantly wait for some great audience,
The smooth sea-tracks that open and close again,
Tracks undiscoverable, indecipherable,
Paths on the earth and tunnels underground,
And bird-tracks in the air—all seemed a part
Of the great labyrinth. And then I'd stumble
In sudden blindness, hasten, almost run,
As if the maze itself were after me
And soon must catch me up. But taking thought,
I'd tell myself, 'You need not hurry. This
Is the firm good earth. All roads lie free before you.'
But my bad spirit would sneer, 'No, do not hurry.
No need to hurry. Haste and delay are equal
In this one world, for there's no exit, none,
No place to come to, and you'll end where you are,
Deep in the centre of the endless maze.'

I could not live if this were not illusion.
It is a world, perhaps; but there's another.
For once in a dream or trance I saw the gods

Each sitting on the top of his mountain-isle,
50   While down below the little ships sailed by,
Toy multitudes swarmed in the harbours, shepherds drove
Their tiny flocks to the pastures, marriage feasts
Went on below, small birthdays and holidays,
Ploughing and harvesting and life and death,
And all permissible, all acceptable,
Clear and secure as in a limpid dream.
But they, the gods, as large and bright as clouds,
Conversed across the sounds in tranquil voices
High in the sky above the untroubled sea,
60   And their eternal dialogue was peace
Where all these things were woven, and this our life
Was as a chord deep in that dialogue,
As easy utterance of harmonious words,
Spontaneous syllables bodying forth a world.

That was the real world; I have touched it once,
And now shall know it always. But the lie,
The maze, the wild-wood waste of falsehood, roads
That run and run and never reach an end,
Embowered in error—I'd be prisoned there
70   But that my soul has birdwings to fly free.

Oh these deceits are strong almost as life.
Last night I dreamt I was in the labyrinth,
And woke far on. I did not know the place.

The Child Dying

Unfriendly friendly universe,
I pack your stars into my purse,
And bid you, bid you so farewell.
That I can leave you, quite go out,
Go out, go out beyond all doubt,
My father says, is the miracle.

You are so great, and I so small:
I am nothing, you are all:
Being nothing, I can take this way.
Oh I need neither rise nor fall,
For when I do not move at all
I shall be out of all your day.

It's said some memory will remain
In the other place, grass in the rain,
Light on the land, sun on the sea,
A flitting grace, a phantom face,
But the world is out. There is no place
Where it and its ghost can ever be.

Father, father, I dread this air
Blown from the far side of despair,
The cold cold corner. What house, what hold,
What hand is there? I look and see
Nothing-filled eternity,
And the great round world grows weak and old.

Hold my hand, oh hold it fast—
I am changing!—until at last
My hand in yours no more will change,
Though yours change on. You here, I there,
So hand in hand, twin-leafed despair—
I did not know death was so strange.

The Combat

It was not meant for human eyes,
That combat on the shabby patch
Of clods and trampled turf that lies
Somewhere beneath the sodden skies
For eye of toad or adder to catch.

And having seen it I accuse
The crested animal in his pride,
Arrayed in all the royal hues
Which hide the claws he well can use
To tear the heart out of the side.

Body of leopard, eagle's head
And whetted beak, and lion's mane,
And frost-grey hedge of feathers spread
Behind—he seemed of all things bred.
I shall not see his like again.

As for his enemy, there came in
A soft round beast as brown as clay;
All rent and patched his wretched skin;
A battered bag he might have been,
Some old used thing to throw away.

Yet he awaited face to face
The furious beast and the swift attack.
Soon over and done. That was no place
Or time for chivalry or for grace.
The fury had him on his back.

And two small paws like hands flew out
To right and left as the trees stood by.
One would have said beyond a doubt
This was the very end of the bout,
But that the creature would not die.

For ere the death-stroke he was gone,
Writhed, whirled, huddled into his den,
Safe somehow there. The fight was done,
And he had lost who had all but won.
But oh his deadly fury then.

A while the place lay blank, forlorn,
Drowsing as in relief from pain.
The cricket chirped, the grating thorn
Stirred, and a little sound was born.
The champions took their posts again.

And all began. The stealthy paw
Slashed out and in. Could nothing save
These rags and tatters from the claw?
Nothing. And yet I never saw
A beast so helpless and so brave.

And now, while the trees stand watching, still
The unequal battle rages there.
The killing beast that cannot kill
Swells and swells in his fury till
You'd almost think it was despair.

The Interrogation

We could have crossed the road but hesitated,
And then came the patrol;
The leader conscientious and intent,
The men surly, indifferent.
While we stood by and waited
The interrogation began. He says the whole
Must come out now, who, what we are,
Where we have come from, with what purpose, whose
Country or camp we plot for or betray.
Question on question.
We have stood and answered through the standing day
And watched across the road beyond the hedge
The careless lovers in pairs go by,
Hand linked in hand, wandering another star,
So near we could shout to them. We cannot choose
Answer or action here,
Though still the careless lovers saunter by
And the thoughtless field is near.

We are on the very edge,
20   Endurance almost done,
          And still the interrogation is going on.

The Good Town

Look at it well. This was the good town once,
Known everywhere, with streets of friendly neighbours,
Street friend to street and house to house. In
          summer
All day the doors stood open; lock and key
Were quaint antiquities fit for museums
With gyves and rusty chains. The ivy grew
From post to post across the prison door.
The yard behind was sweet with grass and flowers,
A place where grave philosophers loved to walk.
10   Old Time that promises and keeps his promise
Was our sole lord indulgent and severe,
Who gave and took away with gradual hand
That never hurried, never tarried, still
Adding, subtracting. These our houses had
Long fallen into decay but that we knew
Kindness and courage can repair time's faults,
And serving him breeds patience and courtesy
In us, light sojourners and passing subjects.
There is a virtue in tranquillity
20   That makes all fitting, childhood and youth and age,
Each in its place.

               Look well. These mounds of rubble,
And shattered piers, half-windows, broken arches
And groping arms were once inwoven in walls
Covered with saints and angels, bore the roof,
Shot up the towering spire. These gaping bridges
Once spanned the quiet river which you see
Beyond that patch of raw and angry earth
Where the new concrete houses sit and stare.

Walk with me by the river. See, the poplars
Still gather quiet gazing on the stream.
The white road winds across the small green hill
And then is lost. These few things still remain.
Some of our houses too, though not what once
Lived there and drew a strength from memory.
Our people have been scattered, or have come
As strangers back to mingle with the strangers
Who occupy our rooms where none can find
The place he knew but settles where he can.
No family now sits at the evening table;
Father and son, mother and child are *out*,
A quaint and obsolete fashion. In our houses
Invaders speak their foreign tongues, informers
Appear and disappear, chance whores, officials
Humble or high, frightened, obsequious,
Sit carefully in corners. My old friends
(Friends ere these great disasters) are dispersed
In parties, armies, camps, conspiracies.
We avoid each other. If you see a man
Who smiles good-day or waves a lordly greeting
Be sure he's a policeman or a spy.
We know them by their free and candid air.

It was not time that brought these things upon us,
But these two wars that trampled on us twice,
Advancing and withdrawing, like a herd
Of clumsy-footed beasts on a stupid errand
Unknown to them or us. Pure chance, pure malice,
Or so it seemed. And when, the first war over,
The armies left and our own men came back
From every point by many a turning road,
Maimed, crippled, changed in body or in mind,
It was a sight to see the cripples come
Out on the fields. The land looked all awry,
The roads ran crooked and the light fell wrong.
Our fields were like a pack of cheating cards
Dealt out at random—all we had to play
In the bad game for the good stake, our life.
We played; a little shrewdness scraped us through.

Then came the second war, passed and repassed,
And now you see our town, the fine new prison,
70   The house-doors shut and barred, the frightened
        faces
Peeping round corners, secret police, informers,
And all afraid of all.

             How did it come?
From outside, so it seemed, an endless source,
Disorder inexhaustible, strange to us,
Incomprehensible. Yet sometimes now
We ask ourselves, we the old citizens:
'Could it have come from us? Was our peace peace?
Our goodness goodness? That old life was easy
And kind and comfortable; but evil is restless
80   And gives no rest to the cruel or the kind.
How could our town grow wicked in a moment?
What is the answer? Perhaps no more than this,
That once the good men swayed our lives, and those
Who copied them took a while the hue of goodness,
A passing loan; while now the bad are up,
And we, poor ordinary neutral stuff,
Not good nor bad, must ape them as we can,
In sullen rage or vile obsequiousness.
Say there's a balance between good and evil
90   In things, and it's so mathematical,
So finely reckoned that a jot of either,
A bare preponderance will do all you need,
Make a town good, or make it what you see.
But then, you'll say, only that jot is wanting,
That grain of virtue. No: when evil comes
All things turn adverse, and we must begin
At the beginning, heave the groaning world
Back in its place again, and clamp it there.
Then all is hard and hazardous. We have seen
100 Good men made evil wrangling with the evil,
Straight minds grown crooked fighting crooked minds.
Our peace betrayed us; we betrayed our peace.
Look at it well. This was the good town once.'

These thoughts we have, walking among our ruins.

Soliloquy

I have seen Alexandria, imperial Rome,
And the sultry backlanes of Jerusalem
One late spring evening thirty years ago
Trouble me still. It was a holy day:
The inns and taverns packed to the very door,
Goods, cattle, families, fellowships, clans;
And some time after a man was crucified,
So it is said, who died for love of the world.
Strange deeds, strange scenes. I have passed through war
    and peace,
10 Watched populations driven along the roads
To emptiness, movements like bird-migrations
Of races and great families, bare at the last,
Equal in destitution. I have felt
Fear in my throat and fury in my heart,
Dreaded the shadow of the waving palm,
The rustling of the lizard, have been caught
In battles where armies shouted foreign cries,
Fought for strange purposes; and in an eddy
Deep in the slaughter once I watched
20 A madman sitting happily in the sand,
Rapt in his world. I have seen more than I know.
I was a brisk young merchant, brazen as youth
When youth is brazen. Now I am old and wait
Here in my country house in quiet Greece.
What have I gathered?

                  I have picked up wisdom lying
Disused about the world, available still,
Employable still, small odds and scraps of wisdom,
A miscellaneous lot that yet makes up
30 A something that is genuine, with a body,
A shape, a character, more than half Platonic
(Greek, should I say?), and yet of practical use.
I have learnt a host of little things, and one
Too great for thinking, scarcely to be borne:

That there's a watershed in human life,
A natural mountain which we have to scale;
And once at the top, our journey all lies downward,
Down the long slope to age and sleep and the end,
(Sadder but easier than the hills of youth,
And sometimes shot with gleams of sunset light).
Oh the air is different on this side of the hill,
The sunset side. And when I breathed it first
I felt dismay so deep and yet so quiet,
It was a silence rather, a sea of silence.
This is my trouble, the common trouble.

I have seen
Troy's harbour deep in the fields with turf grown over
And poppies nodding on the rustic quays;
And temples and curious caverns in the rocks
Scrawled thick with suns and birds and animals,
Fruit, fire and feast, flower-garlanded underworld;
Past reading.

I have learned another lesson:
When life's half done you must give quality
To the other half, else you lose both, lose all.
Select, select: make an anthology
Of what's been given you by bold casual time.
Revise, omit; keep what's significant.
Fill, fill deserted time. Oh there's no comfort
In the wastes of empty time. Provide for age.
Life must be lived; then live. And so I turn
To past experience, watch it being shaped,
But never to its own true shape. However,
I have fitted this or that into the pattern,
Caught sight sometimes of the original
That is myself—should rather be myself—
The soul past price bartered at any price
The moment bids, cheap as the cheapest moment.
I have had such glimpses, made such tentative
Essays to shape my life, have had successes,
Whether real or apparent time may tell,

40

50

60

70

Though there's no bargain you can drive with time.
All this is insufficient.

I have watched
In cheering ports the great fleets setting out,
And on another and a darker day
Returning with disaster at the helm,
Death at the prow—and then the punishments,
The crucifixions on the burning hills,
Hour-long day-long slow death. And once I came
Upon the gaunt-ribbed skeleton of a wreck
Black underneath the toothed black promontory;
Nothing but these to comfort one another,
And the spray and grinding sea.

I have seen such things.
I have begotten life and taken away
Life lent to others. I have thought of death,
And followed Plato to eternity,
Walked in his radiant world; have trod the fields
My fathers' sins have trampled richly down,
Loam warmed by a sun that burns at the world's heart,
Sol of the underworld. My heart is steady,
Beats in my breast and cannot burn or break,
Systole and diastole for seventy years.

Set up the bleak worn day to show our sins,
Old and still ageing, like a flat squat herd
Crawling like sun on wall to the rim of time,
Up the long slope for ever.

Light and praise,
Love and atonement, harmony and peace,
Touch me, assail me; break and make my heart.

The Transfiguration

So from the ground we felt that virtue branch
Through all our veins till we were whole, our wrists
As fresh and pure as water from a well,
Our hands made new to handle holy things,
The source of all our seeing rinsed and cleansed
Till earth and light and water entering there
Gave back to us the clear unfallen world.
We would have thrown our clothes away for lightness,
But that even they, though sour and travel stained,
Seemed, like our flesh, made of immortal substance,
And the soiled flax and wool lay light upon us
Like friendly wonders, flower and flock entwined
As in a morning field. Was it a vision?
Or did we see that day the unseeable
One glory of the everlasting world
Perpetually at work, though never seen
Since Eden locked the gate that's everywhere
And nowhere? Was the change in us alone,
And the enormous earth still left forlorn,
An exile or a prisoner? Yet the world
We saw that day made this unreal, for all
Was in its place. The painted animals
Assembled there in gentle congregations,
Or sought apart their leafy oratories,
Or walked in peace, the wild and tame together,
As if, also for them, the day had come.
The shepherds' hovels shone, for underneath
The soot we saw the stone clean at the heart
As on the starting-day. The refuse heaps
Were grained with that fine dust that made the world;
For he had said, 'To the pure all things are pure,'
And when we went into the town, he with us,
The lurkers under doorways, murderers,
With rags tied round their feet for silence, came
Out of themselves to us and were with us,
And those who hide within the labyrinth
Of their own loneliness and greatness came,

And those entangled in their own devices,
The silent and the garrulous liars, all
Stepped out of their dungeons and were free.
Reality or vision, this we have seen.
If it had lasted but another moment
It might have held for ever! But the world
Rolled back into its place, and we are here,
And all that radiant kingdom lies forlorn,
As if it had never stirred; no human voice
Is heard among its meadows, but it speaks
To itself alone, alone it flowers and shines
And blossoms for itself while time runs on.

But he will come again, it's said, though not
Unwanted and unsummoned; for all things,
Beasts of the field, and woods, and rocks, and seas,
And all mankind from end to end of the earth
Will call him with one voice. In our own time,
Some say, or at a time when time is ripe,
Then he will come, Christ the uncrucified,
Christ the discrucified, his death undone,
His agony unmade, his cross dismantled—
Glad to be so—and the tormented wood
Will cure its hurt and grow into a tree
In a green springing corner of young Eden,
And Judas damned take his long journey backward
From darkness into light and be a child
Beside his mother's knee, and the betrayal
Be quite undone and never more be done.

50

60

Vernon Watkins

from THE BALLAD OF THE MARI LWYD 1941

The Collier

When I was born on Amman hill
A dark bird crossed the sun.
Sharp on the floor the shadow fell;
I was the youngest son.

And when I went to the County School
I worked in a shaft of light.
In the wood of the desk I cut my name:
Dai for Dynamite.

The tall black hills my brothers stood;
Their lessons all were done.
From the door of the school when I ran out
They frowned to watch me run.

The slow grey bells they rung a chime
Surly with grief or age.
Clever or clumsy, lad or lout,
All would look for a wage.

I learnt the valley flowers' names
And the rough bark knew my knees.
I brought home trout from the river
And spotted eggs from the trees.

A coloured coat I was given to wear
Where the lights of the rough land shone.
Still jealous of my favour
The tall black hills looked on.

They dipped my coat in the blood of a kid
And they cast me down a pit,
And although I crossed with strangers
There was no way up from it.

Soon as I went from the County School
I worked in a shaft. Said Jim,
'You will get your chain of gold, my lad,
But not for a likely time.'

And one said, 'Jack was not raised up
When the wind blew out the light
Though he interpreted their dreams
And guessed their fears by night.'

And Tom, he shivered his leper's lamp
For the stain that round him grew;
And I heard mouths pray in the after-damp
When the picks would not break through.

They changed words there in the darkness
And still through my head they run,
And white on my limbs is the linen sheet
And gold on my neck the sun.

from THE LADY WITH THE UNICORN 1948

Sardine Fishers at Daybreak

Lifted on linen, I feel
In the full moon's white lake

Death in the wake of the keel,
Threads that strain and break
Before the breaking of day.
Noise knocked me awake,
Flight of the Milky Way,
Then hammering heels, a wake
Of heels on the cobbled town,
Clogs clattering down
To the harbour, a march of death,
Flight of the lives under breath,
From the shooting light, their race,
Pulled to the meeting-place,
Caught in short nets, they shun,
Gasping, the livid sun.

Snared sunbeams, flashing, show
A forest of masts, a fire
Of colour; and, mounting higher,
Tall rods that flicker and glow
Moored at Concarneau, where
A reflected clock tells time.
Rapier-like they climb
From the bright boats anchored there.
These wait for a priest to bless
Their going; and the folded sails,
Bound for the coast of Wales,
Point, in their idleness,
North, where sardine-boats dress
In nets near the Point each tree;
And octopus-dark below,
Where blood-red tunnies go
Audierne, the silent sea.

Before dawn, hard to discern,
From the jetty, cold as a cairn,
Thumping with motors, go
Ships from Audierne,
And hang their nets low.
Slow from the grey quay, slow,

Without sails they pass.
Then three in a dinghy row
Out on the sea of glass.
One stands in the dinghy, seen
Flinging meal as to fowls.
The moon is white like a queen.
He gives a sign; and with owls'
Noiseless flight they steal
Back to the silent keel.

Flat, flat as a lake
Is the sea, silent, a wonder.
That silence who can break?
They are the silver under
Breath, and all shall die.
Rough hands take
Over the slippery, sly
Sides of the ship blue nets
Of fish that fall in a heap
On the deck, bright winding-sheets
Coiled in the wake of sleep.
Their touch no hand reveals
Through the strange, cold element
Until they fall in creels,
Killed by the daylight, spent.

Where three hundred ships meet,
Miles out at sea, a silent fleet,
Before light breaks, blue nets,
Gossamer, fine as lawn,
Are dropped from their threaded floats,
Dropped from the sardine-boats
By hands familiar with dawn.

From under the waking sea
Ascend the brilliant heads
Of sleep. Mysteriously
I watch them, caught in threads,
Tugged like a silver river,

Hauled by rough hands over
The burdened side of the ship,
Terrified, shuddering, shy
Incarnations of sky,
Hover, tumble down
To the sleek boards, wet and brown
Under a rust-brown sail.
They lie about rope and bale,
Flounder, splash, and are still,
Cast on a mounting hill.

Ah cold, where no two lives meet,
Light's fine needle quivers.
Under sea a white film hovers,
A caul whose haul discovers,
White as a winding-sheet,
Gasping in death, night's lovers,
Flight of hid stars. The sun
Is rising, rising. The sun
Is rising, waking from sleep.
Look, they sparkle and leap,
Vanishing, one by one.
With heaving force they are drawn
Over the spanned ship's sides
By hands grown old with the tides,
And dropped there, trophies of dawn,
Shaken, taken,
Frail, lit, forsaken,
Falling dead at my feet.

Sky is brightening while they are spent.
Four men are standing afresh
While one is crouching, bent.
The crew rip open the tent
Of light. With a knife they gash
The brilliant, awakened sheet.
They are shaking the silver fish.
Caught, I see them flash,
Fastened, glittering, steep

Into blue threads drawn
From darkness, wrung from sleep,
Falling in that bright heap,
Hung in the webs of dawn.

The Feather

I stoop to gather a seabird's feather
Fallen on the beach,
Torn from a beautiful drifting wing;
What can I learn or teach,
Running my finger through the comb
And along the horny quill?
The body it was torn from
Gave out a cry so shrill,
Sailors looked from their white road
To see what help was there.
It dragged the winds to a drop of blood
Falling through drowned air,
Dropping from the sea-hawk's beak,
From frenzied talons sharp;
Now if the words they lost I speak
It must be to that harp
Under the strange, light-headed sea
That bears a straw of the nest.
Unless I make that melody,
How can the dead have rest?

Sheer from wide air to the wilderness
The victim fell, and lay;
The starlike bone is fathomless,
Lost among wind and spray.
This lonely, isolated thing
Trembles amid their sound.
I set my finger on the string
That spins the ages round.
But let it sleep, let it sleep
Where shell and stone are cast;

E*

Its ecstasy the Furies keep,
For nothing here is past.
The perfect into night must fly;
On this the winds agree.
How could a blind rock satisfy
The hungers of the sea?

The Healing of the Leper

O, have you seen the leper healed,
And fixed your eyes upon his look?
There is the book of God revealed,
And God has made no other book.

The withered hand which time interred
Grasps in a moment the unseen.
The word we had not heard, is heard.
What we are then, we had not been.

Plotinus, preaching on heaven's floor.
Could not give praise like that loud cry
Bursting the bondage of death's door;
For we die once; indeed we die.

What Sandro Botticelli found
Rose from the river where we bathe:
Music the air, the stream, the ground;
Music the dove, the rock, the faith:

And all that music whirled upon
The eyes' deep-sighted, burning rays,
Where all the prayers of labours done
Are resurrected into praise.

But look: his face is like a mask
Surrounded by the beat of wings.
Because he knows that ancient task
His true transfiguration springs.

All fires the prophets' words contained
Fly to those eyes, transfixed above.
Their awful precept has remained:
'Be nothing, first; and then, be love'.

Lace-maker

Lined, wrinkled face,
Fingers of Samothrace
Making so secretly move
In a fragile pattern of lace
Your untranslatable love:

Dark, withdrawn from delight,
Under the water-bowl light
On a cushion spread in your room
Pricking the stretch of night
With secrets old as the womb:

Patient, you toil alone.
Eighty years are gone
Since first your fingers tossed
Those bobbins one by one
In a craft that is almost lost.

Flashing in failing skies,
Gay Kitty Fisher's Eyes,
As they call these Buckingham beads,
Restore that far sunrise
To your pensive widow's weeds;

And your shadowing, birdlike hand,
Migrated from a young land,
Brings, like a midnight lark,
Whiter than whitest sand,
Light running out of dark:

Fine sand, too quick to tread,
Crossed by the sea in your head
In a hundred thundering tides
Breaking in foam, the thread
White, unlost, like a bride's

Beautiful, gathered lace,
Foretelling the lover's pace,
That lover of foam, the hot
Sea, for one hour, one place,
One moment, caught in a knot.

No sooner come than gone:
So light, it is not weighed down
By any thought that will stay.
You have seen time's flood that would
    drown
Surpassed in butterflies' play,

Yet intricately surpassed;
For rather you chose to fast
Than sell that delicate stream
Of lace on the altar cast,
A gift, for night to redeem:

Lace, fragile, fine,
In a magic, a moving design,
A silence, in which I see
Through the sea-engendered vine
A glory, not of the sea.

30

40

50

The Butterflies

High, lost in light, they pair,
Butterflies blue, so fair,
Blind in stopped flight,

Twined on a thread,
Then drop where light, effaced,
Shuts, in the dread
Secret of sepalled air,
Their petals chaste.

Hid, meadow-masked from sight,
Hushed near the pulse of light,
They magnify
With round big eye
Antennae'd, that gold place
From which the sky
Seizes their still delight,
Inventing space.

Suddenly they spring up,
Blown from a buttercup,
Alight, elude,
And reunite;
They mingle their blue wings
Dazzling the sight,
Like a blue wind, then stop,
Sit, and are kings.

That crooked life would seem
Vain, did no falling stream
Chime a strange year
Time-changing here,
And yew-tree with no sound,
And murmuring weir,
Catch on a weaver's beam
The thread they wound

Past the farm wall, where grieves
An aspen, whose wild leaves
Toss, where roots brawl
On fosse and wall,
Gathering their green and white,
Strain, feign to fall,

And cast across the eaves
A changing light:

40

A dancing thread, how much
More fragile, hard to touch,
Brighter in flight,
More light than theirs
Or spiders' threads in air.
Fugitive players:
It was a pain to watch —
A twine so fair

Flying, so quickly gone,
Stretching their dalliance on
From plot to plot,
Not to return,
Past hedge and flowering rose,
Falling in turn,
As though the hour had shone
For none but those.

50

Zacchaeus in the Leaves

Silence before
Sound.
Sycamore:

A tree
Predestined to beauty.
Blown leaves. Antiquity.
Light lost. Light found.

The myth above the myth.
The imagined zenith
Of youth in youth.

10

Light on the leaves in wind
Flying. The silver-sequined
Goat-leaf, dark-skinned.

Sycamore leaves; coiled thick,
God-dark, Dionysiac,
The ascending trunk. Pan's music.
The sap made quick.

Wind-gathered sound. The flow
Of lives. Wood-sounds. Wood-hollow.
Hades locked below.

Sap leaps. The springing race
Threading the magic surface
Drops to one place.

A sign to us!
A tree, and then a tree
No more.

Silent Zacchaeus,
Ageless one.
The buried sun,
And the key it bore.

*   *   *

Light found in every age
The leaves of Spring
Fading from lineage,
The seed, the wing.

From what dark scent
Of waters breaking
In night most innocent
Of dead men waking.

From what laid bone
Rose man's belief?

What Sibyl wrote upon
The breaking leaf?

Sibylline words.
The buried lives.
Lost among nesting-birds,
The burden of the leaves.

The myth above the myth,
Pan above Zacchaeus;
Zacchaeus climbing,
Mounted above his youth,
Alone in time
Seeking the heavenly death.

The crooked he had left,
Yes, and the wise,
To climb the tree-trunk,
To sit in a cleft
And see through his eyes
Not what they saw,
Not what they heard,
No leaf, no claw,
No wing, no bird,
But light surpassing
All known green,
As if all drunk
And sober stirred,
Known, unknown,
Where seen, unseen,
Were one alone;
Jesus passing,
The Nazarene.

Lovers embraced
And their eyes were solaced;
But Zacchaeus gripped fast

The tree-branch, crouching,
Watching the myth
Moving, the myth
Move to the zenith
Not found in youth:
'If His eyes see us,
If His eyes see us,
Dazzled above men,
Though we are buried then,
The myth above the truth.'

Who stilled the pipes of Pan?
What marvel weaves
Death, deathless, pagan,
Turning the Sibyl's leaves?

Firm, yet betrayed no more,
The young lie with the young.
Leaves of the sycamore,
Lifted on wind, give tongue:

'I have supported one
In my own right
Who watched the procession,
His eyes full of light.

I can fade now,
My thought heard or unheard.
Did he not leave my bough,
And said no word?'

*   *   *

Slow the procession coming. The drinkers remained
Sitting cross-legged, close to the dead who were chained,
Beggars of light. Only the man in the tree
Looked on the road, and saw where light was ordained.

Among the quick and the dead is the point divine,
Moving; among those talking, the drinkers of wine,
The shuffling of feet, the running of time, the gust
Of windblown leaves, no, not the Muses, the nine,

Have seen the universe race through the leaves and thrill
Because it has found the point of predestined will,
There where the fountain breaks from lips that are dust.
Stop: the great branches are moving. Now they are still.

Dylan Thomas

from DEATHS AND ENTRANCES 1946

The Conversation of Prayer

The conversation of prayers about to be said
By the child going to bed and the man on the stairs
Who climbs to his dying love in her high room,
The one not caring to whom in his sleep he will move
And the other full of tears that she will be dead,

Turns in the dark on the sound they know will arise
Into the answering skies from the green ground,
From the man on the stairs and the child by his bed.
The sound about to be said in the two prayers
For the sleep in a safe land and the love who dies

Will be the same grief flying. Whom shall they calm?
Shall the child sleep unharmed or the man be crying?
The conversation of prayers about to be said
Turns on the quick and the dead, and the man on the stairs
Tonight shall find no dying but alive and warm

In the fire of his care his love in the high room.
And the child not caring to whom he climbs his prayer
Shall drown in a grief as deep as his true grave,
And mark the dark eyed wave, through the eyes of sleep,
Dragging him up the stairs to one who lies dead.

A Refusal to Mourn the Death, by Fire, of a Child in London

Never until the mankind making
Bird beast and flower
Fathering and all humbling darkness
Tells with silence the last light breaking
And the still hour
Is come of the sea tumbling in harness

And I must enter again the round
Zion of the water bead
And the synagogue of the ear of corn
Shall I let pray the shadow of a sound
Or sow my salt seed
In the least valley of sackcloth to mourn

The majesty and burning of the child's death.
I shall not murder
The mankind of her going with a grave truth
Nor blaspheme down the stations of the breath
With any further
Elegy of innocence and youth.

Deep with the first dead lies London's daughter,
Robed in the long friends,
The grains beyond age, the dark veins of her mother,
Secret by the unmourning water
Of the riding Thames.
After the first death, there is no other.

Poem in October

It was my thirtieth year to heaven
Woke to my hearing from harbour and neighbour wood
And the mussel pooled and the heron
Priested shore

The morning beckon
With water praying and call of seagull and rook
And the knock of sailing boats on the net webbed wall
Myself to set foot
That second
In the still sleeping town and set forth.

My birthday began with the water-
Birds and the birds of the winged trees flying my name
Above the farms and the white horses
And I rose
In rainy autumn
And walked abroad in a shower of all my days.
High tide and the heron dived when I took the road
Over the border
And the gates
Of the town closed as the town awoke.

A springful of larks in a rolling
Cloud and the roadside bushes brimming with whistling
Blackbirds and the sun of October
Summery
On the hill's shoulder,
Here were fond climates and sweet singers suddenly
Come in the morning where I wandered and listened
To the rain wringing
Wind blow cold
In the wood faraway under me.

Pale rain over the dwindling harbour
And over the sea wet church the size of a snail
With its horns through mist and the castle
Brown as owls
But all the gardens
Of spring and summer were blooming in the tall tales
Beyond the border and under the lark full cloud.
There could I marvel
My birthday
Away but the weather turned around.

It turned away from the blithe country
And down the other air and the blue altered sky
Streamed again a wonder of summer
With apples
Pears and red currants
And I saw in the turning so clearly a child's
Forgotten mornings when he walked with his mother
Through the parables
Of sun light
50   And the legends of the green chapels

And the twice told fields of infancy
That his tears burned my cheeks and his heart moved in
        mine.
These were the woods the river and sea
Where a boy
In the listening
Summertime of the dead whispered the truth of his joy
To the trees and the stones and the fish in the tide.
And the mystery
Sang alive
60   Still in the water and singingbirds.

And there could I marvel my birthday
Away but the weather turned around. And the true
Joy of the long dead child sang burning
In the sun.
It was my thirtieth
Year to heaven stood there then in the summer noon
Though the town below lay leaved with October blood.
O may my heart's truth
Still be sung
70   On this high hill in a year's turning.

The Side of the Truth

(for Llewelyn)

This side of the truth,
You may not see, my son,
King of your blue eyes
In the blinding country of youth,
That all is undone,
Under the unminding skies,
Of innocence and guilt
Before you move to make
One gesture of the heart or head,
Is gathered and spilt
Into the winding dark
Like the dust of the dead.

Good and bad, two ways
Of moving about your death
By the grinding sea,
King of your heart in the blind days,
Blow away like breath,
Go crying through you and me
And the souls of all men
Into the innocent
Dark, and the guilty dark, and good
Death, and bad death, and then
In the last element
Fly like the stars' blood,

Like the sun's tears,
Like the moon's seed, rubbish
And fire, the flying rant
Of the sky, king of your six years.
And the wicked wish,
Down the beginning of plants
And animals and birds,
Water and light, the earth and sky,
Is cast before you move,

10

20

30

And all your deeds and words,
Each truth, each lie,
Die in unjudging love.

To Others than You

Friend by enemy I call you out.

You with a bad coin in your socket,
You my friend there with a winning air
Who palmed the lie on me when you looked
Brassily at my shyest secret,
Enticed with twinkling bits of the eye
Till the sweet tooth of my love bit dry,
Rasped at last, and I stumbled and sucked,
Whom now I conjure to stand as thief
In the memory worked by mirrors,
With unforgettably smiling act,
Quickness of hand in the velvet glove
And my whole heart under your hammer,
Were once such a creature, so gay and frank
A desireless familiar
I never thought to utter or think
While you displaced a truth in the air.

That though I loved them for their faults
As much as for their good,
My friends were enemies on stilts
With their heads in a cunning cloud.

The Hunchback in the Park

The hunchback in the park
A solitary mister
Propped between trees and water

10

20

From the opening of the garden lock
That lets the trees and water enter
Until the Sunday sombre bell at dark

Eating bread from a newspaper
Drinking water from the chained cup
That the children filled with gravel
0   In the fountain basin where I sailed my ship
Slept at night in a dog kennel
But nobody chained him up.

Like the park birds he came early
Like the water he sat down
And Mister they called Hey mister
The truant boys from the town
Running when he had heard them clearly
On out of sound

Past lake and rockery
0   Laughing when he shook his paper
Hunchbacked in mockery
Through the loud zoo of the willow groves
Dodging the park keeper
With his stick that picked up leaves.

And the old dog sleeper
Alone between nurses and swans
While the boys among willows
Made the tigers jump out of their eyes
To roar on the rockery stones
30   And the groves were blue with sailors

Made all day until bell time
A woman figure without fault
Straight as a young elm
Straight and tall from his crooked bones
That she might stand in the night
After the locks and chains

All night in the unmade park
After the railings and shrubberies
The birds the grass the trees the lake
And the wild boys innocent as strawberries
Had followed the hunchback
To his kennel in the dark.

A Winter's Tale

It is a winter's tale
That the snow blind twilight ferries over the lakes
And floating fields from the farm in the cup of the vales,
Gliding windless through the hand folded flakes,
The pale breath of cattle at the stealthy sail,

And the stars falling cold,
And the smell of hay in the snow, and the far owl
Warning among the folds, and the frozen hold
Flocked with the sheep white smoke of the farm house cowl
10 In the river wended vales where the tale was told.

Once when the world turned old
On a star of faith pure as the drifting bread,
As the food and flames of the snow, a man unrolled
The scrolls of fire that burned in his heart and head,
Torn and alone in a farm house in a fold

Of fields. And burning then
In his firelit island ringed by the winged snow
And the dung hills white as wool and the hen
Roosts sleeping chill till the flame of the cock crow
20 Combs through the mantled yards and the morning men

Stumble out with their spades,
The cattle stirring, the mousing cat stepping shy,
The puffed birds hopping and hunting, the milkmaids
Gentle in their clogs over the fallen sky,
And all the woken farm at its white trades,

He knelt, he wept, he prayed,
By the spit and the black pot in the log bright light
And the cup and the cut bread in the dancing shade,
In the muffled house, in the quick of night,
At the point of love, forsaken and afraid.

He knelt on the cold stones,
He wept from the crest of grief, he prayed to the veiled sky
May his hunger go howling on bare white bones
Past the statues of the stables and the sky roofed sties
And the duck pond glass and the blinding byres alone

Into the home of prayers
And fires where he should prowl down the cloud
Of his snow blind love and rush in the white lairs.
His naked need struck him howling and bowed
Though no sound flowed down the hand folded air

But only the wind strung
Hunger of birds in the fields of the bread of water, tossed
In high corn and the harvest melting on their tongues.
And his nameless need bound him burning and lost
When cold as snow he should run the wended vales among

The rivers mouthed in night,
And drown in the drifts of his need, and lie curled caught
In the always desiring centre of the white
Inhuman cradle and the bride bed forever sought
By the believer and the hurled outcast of light.

Deliver him, he cried,
By losing him all in love, and cast his need
Alone and naked in the engulfing bride,
Never to flourish in the fields of the white seed
Or flower under the time dying flesh astride.

Listen. The minstrels sing
In the departed villages. The nightingale,
Dust in the buried wood, flies on the grains of her wings

And spells on the winds of the dead his winter's tale.
60 The voice of the dust of water from the withered spring

Is telling. The wizened
Stream with bells and baying water bounds. The dew rings
On the gristed leaves and the long gone glistening
Parish of snow. The carved mouths in the rock are wind swept
    strings.
Time sings through the intricately dead snow drop. Listen.

It was a hand or sound
In the long ago land that glided the dark door wide
And there outside on the bread of the ground
A she bird rose and rayed like a burning bride.
70 A she bird dawned, and her breast with snow and scarlet
    downed.

Look. And the dancers move
On the departed, snow bushed green, wanton in moon light
As a dust of pigeons. Exulting, the grave hooved
Horses, centaur dead, turn and tread the drenched white
Paddocks in the farms of birds. The dead oak walks for love.

The carved limbs in the rock
Leap, as to trumpets. Calligraphy of the old
Leaves is dancing. Lines of age on the stones weave in a
    flock.
And the harp shaped voice of the water's dust plucks in a
    fold
80 Of fields. For love, the long ago she bird rises. Look.

And the wild wings were raised
Above her folded head, and the soft feathered voice
Was flying through the house as though the she bird praised
And all the elements of the slow fall rejoiced
That a man knelt alone in the cup of the vales,

In the mantle and calm,
By the spit and the black pot in the log bright light.

140

And the sky of birds in the plumed voice charmed
Him up and he ran like a wind after the kindling flight
Past the blind barns and byres of the windless farm.

In the poles of the year
When black birds died like priests in the cloaked hedge row
And over the cloth of counties the far hills rode near,
Under the one leaved trees ran a scarecrow of snow
And fast through the drifts of the thickets antlered like deer,

Rags and prayers down the knee-
Deep hillocks and loud on the numbed lakes,
All night lost and long wading in the wake of the she-
Bird through the times and lands and tribes of the slow flakes.
Listen and look where she sails the goose plucked sea,

The sky, the bird, the bride,
The cloud, the need, the planted stars, the joy beyond
The fields of seed and the time dying flesh astride,
The heavens, the heaven, the grave, the burning font.
In the far ago land the door of his death glided wide,

And the bird descended.
On a bread white hill over the cupped farm
And the lakes and floating fields and the river wended
Vales where he prayed to come to the last harm
And the home of prayers and fires, the tale ended.

The dancing perishes
On the white, no longer growing green, and, minstrel dead,
The singing breaks in the snow shoed villages of wishes
That once cut the figures of birds on the deep bread
And over the glazed lakes skated the shapes of fishes

Flying. The rite is shorn
Of nightingale and centaur dead horse. The springs wither
Back. Lines of age sleep on the stones till trumpeting dawn.
Exultation lies down. Time buries the spring weather
That belled and bounded with the fossil and the dew reborn.

For the bird lay bedded
In a choir of wings, as though she slept or died,
And the wings glided wide and he was hymned and wedded,
And through the thighs of the engulfing bride,
The woman breasted and the heaven headed

Bird, he was brought low,
Burning in the bride bed of love, in the whirl-
Pool at the wanting centre, in the folds
Of paradise, in the spun bud of the world.
130 And she rose with him flowering in her melting snow.

In my Craft or Sullen Art

In my craft or sullen art
Exercised in the still night
When only the moon rages
And the lovers lie abed
With all their griefs in their arms,
I labour by singing light
Not for ambition or bread
Or the strut and trade of charms
On the ivory stages
10 But for the common wages
Of their most secret heart.

Not for the proud man apart
From the raging moon I write
On these spindrift pages
Nor for the towering dead
With their nightingales and psalms
But for the lovers, their arms
Round the griefs of the ages,
Who pay no praise or wages
20 Nor heed my craft or art.

Fern Hill

Now as I was young and easy under the apple boughs
About the lilting house and happy as the grass was green,
 The night above the dingle starry,
  Time let me hail and climb
 Golden in the heydays of his eyes,
And honoured among wagons I was prince of the apple towns
And once below a time I lordly had the trees and leaves
  Trail with daisies and barley
 Down the rivers of the windfall light.

10 And as I was green and carefree, famous among the barns
About the happy yard and singing as the farm was home,
 In the sun that is young once only,
  Time let me play and be
 Golden in the mercy of his means,
And green and golden I was huntsman and herdsman, the
  calves
Sang to my horn, the foxes on the hills barked clear and cold,
  And the sabbath rang slowly
 In the pebbles of the holy streams.

All the sun long it was running, it was lovely, the hay
20 Fields high as the house, the tunes from the chimneys, it
  was air
 And playing, lovely and watery
  And fire green as grass.
 And nightly under the simple stars
As I rode to sleep the owls were bearing the farm away,
All the moon long I heard, blessed among stables, the
  nightjars
 Flying with the ricks, and the horses
  Flashing into the dark.

And then to awake, and the farm, like a wanderer white
With the dew, come back, the cock on his shoulder: it was all
30 Shining, it was Adam and maiden,
  The sky gathered again
 And the sun grew round that very day.

So it must have been after the birth of the simple light
In the first, spinning place, the spellbound horses walking
    warm
    Out of the whinnying green stable
      On to the fields of praise.

And honoured among foxes and pheasants by the gay house
Under the new made clouds and happy as the heart was long,
    In the sun born over and over,
      I ran my heedless ways,
40
    My wishes raced through the house high hay
And nothing I cared, at my sky blue trades, that time allows
In all his tuneful turning so few and such morning songs
    Before the children green and golden
      Follow him out of grace,

Nothing I cared, in the lamb white days, that time would
    take me
Up to the swallow thronged loft by the shadow of my hand,
    In the moon that is always rising,
      Nor that riding to sleep
50
    I should hear him fly with the high fields
And wake to the farm forever fled from the childless land.
Oh as I was young and easy in the mercy of his means,
    Time held me green and dying
    Though I sang in my chains like the sea.

Norman Nicholson

from FIVE RIVERS 1944

Rockferns

On quarry walls the spleenwort spreads
Its green zipfasteners and black threads,
And pinches tight its unfurled purses
In every crevice with the cresses,
As if a blast of dynamite
Had spattered it upon the slate
That where the bluestone spine was broken
Spores might penetrate and quicken.
For in the fractures of the rock
Roots dig further than a pick,
As, though the sinews may not feel it,
The worm probes deeper than the bullet.
When this pen is dropped, my hand
May thrust up in a buckler frond,
And then my crushed and calcined bones
Prove better soil than arid stones.
Why need I fear the bursting bomb
Or whatsoever death should come,
If brain and bowels be cast forth
Splintered to spleenwort on the earth?
And if a subtler part may cruise
Twice round the sun and Betelgeuse,
My soul shall detonate on high
And plant itself in cracks of sky.

0

20

Waiting for Spring 1943

A grey wind blows
Through the woods, and the birches are bare,
And the hazel crooks its catkins tight as a starling's claws;
But out in the fields where the dyker hacks the branches
Of purple willow and elder and wrenches
The trunks square to the run of the hedge, there
The yellow lamb's-tails dangle in the frosty air.

So also we
On the perimeter and fringe of war,
₁₀ Open to the sunlight and the wind from the western sea,
Wounded by the knife of winter, still
Feel the bright blood rise to bear
White and daring blossom, fledged before
The seabirds leave the ploughland or the snow leaves the fell.

Let us not forget
Those in whom autumn dug deep furrows of pain,
Those to whom winter has been the kindliest season yet,
The snow their only eiderdown, the frost
Their only morphia; they will not greet again
₂₀ The sap that stings in the bone, nor the bird on the nest
That hatches globes of suffering in the probing rain.

Blood flows back
Into the frozen hand with pain,
And children whimper as the wind flogs them again awake.
To those defeated by the winter's cold
Spring is a terrible season, atonement not to be told
To us in our temperate valleys, who scarcely have begun
To feel the anger of love beneath the conquering sun.

The Evacuees

Four years ago
They came to this little town
Carrying their bundles—women who did not know
Where the sky would lie when their babies were born,
    mothers
With children, children with sisters and brothers,
Children with schoolmates, and frightened children alone.
They saw the strangers at the station, the sea-mist on the hill,
In the windless waiting days when the walls of Poland fell.

Winter came
And the wind did not rise; the sky
Withheld its threat of thunderbolt or bomb.
The women were lonely. Thoughts began to bend
To Northumbrian voices high as a seagull's cry,
To the smell of the North Sea in the streets, the foggy air,
The fish-shops and the neighbours. The tide of fear
Flowed back, leaving weary empty sand.

The women returned
To the Tyneside husbands and the Tyneside coal,
And most of the children followed. Others stayed and
    learned
The Cumberland vowels, took strangers for their friends,
Went home for holidays at first, then not at all,
Accepted in the aisle the bishop's hands,
Won scholarships and badges, and were known
One with the indigenous children of the town.

Four years ago
They came, and in four childhood years
The memory shrivels and the muscles grow.
The little girl who wept on the platform then
Now feels her body blossom like the trees,
Discovers tennis, poetry and flowers,
And under the dripping larches in the rain
Knows the first experiment of a kiss.

Naaman

So this is the river! Cold and still as steel,
Curved round the banks and boulders. Small cascades
Are bent like blades of ploughs and stand as stiffly.
Unceasing movement now is grey and steady
As the dead stone. The roots of thorns
Are plated with the wetness, and lichens nailed
On the rocks like lead. There's not a clipping,
Even, of a ragwort's faded hair
Left in this winter water. This is the river;
This is where I've come! For days I travelled
With my bones groaning at the ruts in the road
And the pain gnawing them. Then from a hut,
A pile of slates half-tumbled into scree,
A lad came out, a red-haired lout,
Chewing a stalk of dry brown grass. He said
The old man said for me to please
Wash my hands in the river. That was all.
He went off spitting the grass into the mud.
So here I am. This is the river. I would have climbed
The highest mountain with the knuckles of my knees
Grinding like a pestle in their sockets. I would have knelt
Hour after hour, my forehead spliced with prayer,
My hands holding my skull. Are not the lowland streams
Wider and purer and cleaner? Would not the tap
Give a better lather than this rocky gutter? I was a fool
To come—let me be fully a fool.
Let the old man have his way, and I'll return
With a bitter shell of scorn to guard my pain.
It's slippery here. The water's in my boots.
Damn boots and water. Come, boy, give me a towel.

148

To a Child Before Birth

This summer is your perfect summer. Never will the skies
So stretched and strident be with blue
As these you do not see; never will the birds surprise
With such light flukes the ferns and fences
As these you do not hear. This year the may
Smells like rum-butter, and day by day
The petals slip from the cups like lover's hands,
Tender and tired and satisfied. This year the haws
Will form as your fingers form, and when in August
The sun first stings your eyes,
The fruit will be red as brick and free to the throstles.
Oh but next year the may
Will have its old smell of plague about it; next year
The songs of the birds be selfish, the skies have rain;
Next year the apples will be tart again.
But do not always grieve
For the unseen summer. Perfection is not the land you leave,
It is the pole you measure from; it gives
Geography to your ways and wanderings.
What is your perfection is another's pain;
And because she in impossible season loves
So in her blood for you the bright bird sings.

Across the Estuary

I

The fog floats in with the tide and lies on the mosses,
Branching up the channels like the veins of an old man's
    hand.
The world of field and farm, the woods and the
    embankment,
Are blurred away like figures on a slate;
Here, under the canvas of the fog,
Is only sand, and the dead, purple turf,

And gulleys in the mud where now the water
Thrusts flabby fingers. The wild geese
Feed beneath the mist, grey and still as sheep,
And cormorants curl black question-marks
Above the threshold of the sea.
                                    Here is the track:
The ruts of cartwheels filled with water, the dark
Brogs of broom. Unseen, a curlew calls—
A shadow slipping through the rippling mist;
Byzantine domes of foam sail up the gutters.
But now—where is the track? where are the ruts?
    The broom
Skulks back into the dark, and every footstep,
Dug deep in mud, draws water through the heels.
Each step goes wrong. Here, forward—deep, the sand
Shifts under foot like scree. Backward—deeper.
Stand still then—squids of sand
Wrap suckers round my feet. The tide
Tops the rim of the gulleys, and the mist
Tightens its cold, wet nets about my throat.

                    II
It is not the eyes of the past
That stare through the mist,
But the eyes that belong to now.

It is not the faces of a dream
That bulge through the gloom,
But the faces of the waking sight.

It is not the voices of the dead
That leave the word unsaid,
But the voices of those who live.
                    III

Thigh-deep in fresh water
I waded the channel
Before the ebb turned.
Do not ask where
Foot first stepped away
From turf to mud,
From dry sand to quicksand;

Oh do not ask where
When foot was bare,
Wings bright in the air
And the sun spinning there,
The wind in my hair,
The unimaginable, rare
Flabbergasting world
Uncurling like a fern,
Unfurling like a flag,
Do not ask where
Foot turned from the ruts,
For my eyes were on the sky
And the wide stripes
Of light above the sea.
And do not ask now
How came I here—
My footsteps veer
Back into the mist,
A bird-track of pools
Oozing like wells
And losing shape
As the sides dissolve.
The past slides
Like sand beneath my feet,
But the past is forgiven—
The unconfessable sins
Of hand and brain and eye,
Murder, rape and lie,
Are washed by the river
To the salvaging brine.
It is not then but now
That tightens like mist about me:
Not how I came
But where I am,
Now what I was,
Nor how I grew
From that to this,
But merely
My being I.

8 0 The tide spreads across the marsh; a six-inch rise
Of water covers miles of sedge and plantain;
Gulleys and gutters are confiscated now
Into the grey acreage of the sea; for a while
The inevasible choice of wrong and less wrong
Is forgotten or deferred. The fog
Is rent like calico, and the sun lets down its ropes,
Yellow, frayed and tangled; gulls and sea-pies
Fly up the estuary, shelducks jangle; but
There is no sign of traveller on the flat waters.

Silecroft Shore

I

Beauty is simple
As a stone, smooth,
Worn into one
Movement, the curve
Still as the orbit
A star loops through.

Stone is simple
As bone which hand,
Shoulder or arm
1 0 Rims round. Bone
Is smoother than skin,
Rounder than flesh.
Under the teaseled
Mesh of hair
Bone is bare
As thought without words,
Pure as desire
Without image, end
Without world.

Stone is the earth's
Cool skeleton,
And bone the rock
That flesh builds on.

II

I walk among the cobbles by the shore:
Not here the nap of turf, the nibs of marram,
Twiddled like compasses by the wind, describing arcs
On the white sand; not here the rockpools and the sea
Spleenwort and the underwater ferns. Instead,
The shingle grinds its teeth beneath my tread,
The pebbles squeak and squelch as I kick among them,
Dark and wet and salty as mussel shells.
Above the wrack I pick a stone,
Bone-dry, black and bare, no seaweed shavings
Nor barnacles' little volcanoes bursting from its flanks:
An indigo mud-stone, from Skiddaw or Black Combe,
Snapped off the rocks and carried to the sea
In the pockets of the ice, its sides planed flat
To long unequal rhomboids; then
Shaken daily in the dice-box of the surf,
Hammered, filed and sandpapered, its roughnesses
            are rounded,
And what was once a chip, a sliver of slate,
Becomes a whole, self-axelled and self-bounded,
Grained like a bird's-egg and simple as a raindrop,
A molecule of beauty. The sea spurge
Feathers green, dripping sticky sap,
The quick ring-plover shifts and disappears
Like a puddle in the sun, and the stones stay
Perfect and purposeful, acknowledging no way
Other of being than this.

III

I lie along the axis of the world.
    My feet are the poles; the ice
    Chisels my shins; my arms are curled
About the tropics where the mid-ribs splice

The continents together. Naked—though
    Shaggy with larches at the fork—
    I seem, and feel the cold scurf snow
On hair as black as heather in the dark

And hidden armpits of the mountains. Bone
    Splinters along the skyline, bare
60   As fortitude, and wind and rain
Gimlet and slice beneath the lathered air.

High from the alps the blood-red rivers fall,
    Veining the snow, and gouging deep
    Cañons in granophyr and shale.
As the old miners wrought with feather, stope

And mallet, so the ice and weather crack
    The sockets of the rocks, and boulders
    Chock up the gulleys, and the slates flake,
And what the green ice breaks the grey snow solders.

70   In warm savannahs of forgetfulness
    The rivers run maroon with blood;
    They flow where brine corrodes my eyes,
And silt the blinded grottoes of my head.

Now brown about my brow settles the mud;
    The ordovician creatures crawl;
    Across the delta corals spread,
Blooming like rhododendrons; fern and shell

Are stamped in sand like heads on coins. Oh now
    Heavy the years, the mud; the rain
80   Fills, drop by drop, a neapless sea,
And centuries fall slowly, grain by grain.

IV

An old man sat in a waterfall
    And the water dripped through his hair;
    His voice was green as a sea-pie's call:

'Come weeds, and turf my skull,
For my hair is loosed by the bite of the beck,—
    Soon my head will be bare;
    I'll have no pride at all.

'Come wagtail, water-ousel sing
    And bubble in my throat;
Come water-rat skulk in my breast,
My flesh shall be your winter coat;
Come water-hen and make your nest
    In hollows of my ribs;
There you'll find a place to play,
For life has rotted my heart away.'

The old man sat in the waterfall
And the water turned his skin to bone.
Stalactites hung from his chin like a beard;
    His shoulders were shelled with stone.
And leaves in autumn drop from tall
Arthritic thorn-trees by the limestone wall
On the old stone man in the waterfall.

V

Bone is simple
As memory, cool
As water that flows
Over jowl and brow
In the pools of sleep;
Drip by drip
Thoughts bulge and fall
Perfect as the world
Curled about them,
Bent on the water's eyeball. Oh!
From what rains, from what clouds,
From what seas, from what streams
Dribble the ghosts
That flood my dreams?

Memory flows
Cool round the bone,

Glazing the white
Like porcelain. Gaze
On the youthful bone,
That bending spine
And rotting teeth
Made in a cradle.
And the bone says:
'It is not I
That bears the daisy head,
But the limestone generations of the dead.'

Memory is beautiful
As a stone, simple
As a sample of mountain,
A handful of hill.
Oh! cobble on the shore
Can you not remember
What you were before
The valleys were brought low?
Can you not forget
What it is to never know

Rock turning slowly
Back into rock
Long to-days ago?

Afterword

With the end of hostilities in 1945 there was, for a variety of reasons already mentioned, a marked slackening of interest in poetry, and this trend continued well into the early 1950s. Alun Lewis, Keith Douglas and Sidney Keyes, three of the most promising poets of the war years, had been killed on active service; Henry Reed and others had turned their attention to different forms of literature; many of the poets who had emerged during the 1940s were still writing; by the end of the decade publishers were inclined to ignore the younger poets and to make available only the work of established writers. This may explain why several of the new poets of the 1950s were introduced to the public by means of pamphlet collections published by such small presses as the Fantasy Press of Oxford (Kingsley Amis, Elizabeth Jennings, and Thom Gunn), the Hand and Flower Press of Aldington, Kent· (Charles Causley, Thomas Blackburn and Michael Hamburger), the Marvell Press of Hull (Philip Larkin, though *The Less Deceived* was a fully bound volume), and the Fine Art Department of Reading University (John Wain and Kingsley Amis).

Although Dylan Thomas wrote very few poems after the appearance of his *Deaths and Entrances* (1946), he continued to exercise a growing influence over poets throughout the English-speaking world. Edwin Muir, Robert Graves, and Vernon Watkins steadily enhanced their reputations, Edith Sitwell came under fire from a few of the younger critics at the universities, but taken as a whole the early 1950s were quite undistinguished. Indeed, it seemed as if the poets of the time, disheartened by their dwindling public, had found the events of the preceding decade, or the enervating effects of the British Welfare State, all too much for them.

With the advantages of hindsight, of course, it is possible to see that new attitudes to poetry, reflecting the reactions of some of the younger poets to the current social situation, were in fact already being formulated; and to trace subsequent developments back to their apparent starting-point. For instance, in 1950 *Penguin New Writing* printed an article by John Wain on William Empson, at that time somewhat neglected as a poet. One can clearly discern the influence of Empson on the early work of John Wain, A. Alvarez, Jonathan Price, George MacBeth and others— an influence operating strongly enough by 1952 to induce G. S. Fraser and Iain Fletcher to attach the label 'Neo-Empsonians' to a number of the contributors to their *Springtime* anthology. The death of Dylan Thomas in 1953 seemed to spark off a controversy between those who regarded Thomas as an important figure and those who deplored his influence. According to John Press in *Rule and Energy* (1963), 'it was, therefore, understandable that a young poet after the war should feel obliged to choose between the poetic worlds of Thomas and Empson, to commit himself to one of them as an act of faith'.

But it was not until late in 1954 that the new fashion in poetry hit the headlines of *The Spectator*, when J. D. Scott announced the arrival of 'The Movement' on the literary scene: 'One day we wake up to this change. Why on one day rather than another? . . . The answer is that nothing dates literary fashions so certainly as the emergence of a new movement, and within the last year or so, signs are multiplying that such a thing is, once again, emerging.' As has been observed in the Foreword to the present volume, new poets often form groups of one kind or another in order to secure a sympathetic hearing and usually call attention to themselves by denouncing the ideas or styles of their immediate predecessors. It was perhaps inevitable, then, that the Movement poets should attack both the political preoccupations of the 1930s and the romantic trends of the 1940s, but there can be no doubt that, despite the various differences in style and treatment, many of the younger poets (and particularly those attached to universities) had certain characteristics in common although they were not all personally acquainted. The Movement 'as well as being anti-phoney, is anti-wet; sceptical, robust, ironic, prepared to be as comfortable as possible in a wicked commercial threatened world which doesn't look anyway as if it is going to be changed much by a couple of handfuls of young English writers'. The Movement anthology, *New Lines*, edited by Robert Conquest and containing the work of nine poets (Elizabeth Jennings, Amis, Wain, Larkin, Gunn, Enright, Holloway, Davie and Conquest), appeared in 1956.

As if to demonstrate that *all* the younger poets were not in sympathy with the ideas of the Movement, it was followed almost immediately by a rival anthology, *Mavericks*, edited by Dannie Abse and Howard Sergeant, presenting the work of nine poets outside the Movement who were 'making a valid attempt to grapple with problems beyond those of technique (important though these may be) and to communicate, lucidly and honestly, what they feel to be significant experience'.

It is beyond the scope of this volume to consider the relative merits of the opposing Movement and Maverick poets, other than to remark that the conflict between them was something more than rivalry between schools of poets, it was concerned with ideas fundamental to poetry, and as John Press has observed (*Rule and Energy*), 'the dialogue between them has moulded and defined the history of poetry in England since the war'. For Mr Press it was a conflict between two dominant voices: 'The voice which argues, teaches, sets in order; and the voice which chants, affirms, prophesies.' For Robert Shaw, it emphasized the distinction between two types of poetry—that of poets who have been 'content to use the verbal resources they inherited—but for their own sake, rather than for their original purpose of extending our awareness' and that 'which is much more aware of the distinctive qualities of contemporary society and in communicating this consciousness it tests the techniques passed down to the full' (*Flashpoint*, 1964). For John Holloway, it was a clash between two available languages of poetry: the language that 'points towards a dry, even cagey intelligence' and that which 'points towards inspiration or abandon' (*Symposium on English Poetry since 1945* in *London Magazine*). For Alvarez it was simply a continuation of the 'classics *v* romantics battle'.

Notes

The notes in this edition are intended to serve the needs of overseas students as well as those of English-born users. Accordingly, all relevant *information* not likely to be readily available has been noted; *interpretation* has been left to the reader—except when its avoidance seemed inseparable from withholding information (where the poet may have used language or imagery in a way peculiar to himself). Line references are given in italic numerals.

Textual Notes

Alun Lewis

From *Raiders Dawn* (1942)

RAIDERS' DAWN

4. Peter and Paul: Quite apart from the obvious connection between the falling of 'civilised centuries' and the failing influence of Christianity (i.e. the reference to the two great apostles of Christianity, St Peter and St Paul), there would appear to be an indirect reference to the infants' game with the fingers, called 'Two Little Dicky Birds', in which a piece of paper is stuck on each index finger, one being called Peter and the other Paul; by sleight of hand during the course of the game the two papers are concealed and seem to disappear. There is also a similarity of rhythm between the first stanza of the poem and 'Two Little Dicky Birds'.

14. *on a charred chair:* the poem is about the effects of an air-raid.

ALL DAY IT HAS RAINED

2. *bell-tents:* large tents, roughly bell-shaped and made of canvas, used by the army when in camp.

7. *guy-ropes:* ropes securing the tents to pegs hammered in the ground. In wet weather guy-ropes are usually slackened, since they become taut and may easily snap.

14. *woodbine:* a cheap cigarette of the 'wild woodbine' brand.

18. *herded refugees:* refugees from war-stricken Europe were housed in refugee camps, hence herded.

28. *Sheet and Steep:* Villages in Hampshire. During the first year of the war Lewis was a sapper in the Engineers stationed in Hampshire.

THE PUBLIC GARDENS

4. *rococo:* a style of decoration distinguished by ornament in imitation of rockwork, shells, foliage and scrolls massed together: oldfashioned.

12. *reciting the liturgy of vexations:* a liturgy is a collection of prescribed forms for public worship; a ritual. The implication here is that the wealthy older lady makes a ritual of complaining.

14. *demi-Parnassian:* Parnassian means 'belonging to poetry'; there is something poetic about the beautiful companion as the sunshine plays on her dark hair.

22. *my khaki, my crude trade:* the poet is in army uniform (khaki colour) and his trade that of a soldier.

TO EDWARD THOMAS

40. *Helen:* Edward Thomas's wife.

54. *you possessed that hinted land:* Edward Thomas was killed at Arras in the First World War (1917)

POST-SCRIPT: FOR GWENO: Gweno is Lewis's wife. From *Ha! Ha! Among the Trumpets* (1945)

INFANTRY

5. *gambits:* various openings in the game of chess, in which a pawn or minor piece is risked to gain some advantage.

12. black market: since certain foods and articles were rationed during war time, an illegitimate trade in scarce goods quickly developed, which was known as the 'black market', on which it was possible to buy rationed or scarce goods at a grossly inflated price. Lewis suggests here that the soldiers themselves are commodities of a more sinister black market.

14. unction: the act of anointing with oil as a rite or ceremonial, as in consecration or dedication, especially in the Roman Catholic Church and Greek Orthodox Church, but in the former only when the person so anointed is in danger of death. 'Rum's holy unction' refers to the soldier's rum ration, before taking part in an attack.

SONG

4. Naked in Eden: a comparison with the innocence of Adam and Eve in the garden of Eden.

GOODBYE

5. shilling in the gas: in the gas meter regulating the supply to the gas fire.

10. mummy-cloths: the cloths in which Egyptian mummies were wrapped.

29. the emerald: an emerald engagement ring.

KARANJE VILLAGE. Lewis was posted to India with the South Wales Borderers.

15. sari: garment worn by Hindu women.

18. Vishnu of stone: a stone representation of Vishnu, one of the principal Hindu deities, usually identified with the supreme deity and regarded as the world-preserver. In his unpublished journal Lewis describes finding a granite Buddha in similar circumstances.

27. matrix: that which contains and gives shape or form to anything; the womb.

THE MAHRATTA GHATS

10. Siva: Hindu deity to whom are attributed the powers of reproduction and dissolution.

23. bumming: a bum, in American slang, is a tramp or loafer; hence a beggar is 'bumming'.

THE PEASANTS

12. The peasants watch them die: although leading such circumscribed lives, the peasants are nevertheless free to observe the fate of soldiers, who are victims of history and the necessity of war.

Keith Douglas

From *Collected Poems* (1951)

TIME EATING

1. flowers for his food: the flowers are subject to time and die in the Autumn. The poem considers time both as a destroyer and as a creator.

11. ruminative: a double meaning intended here—turning over in the mouth, and meditative.

12. masticate: since 'to masticate' is to chew perhaps this is not the precise word. Douglas uses it in the sense of dissolution.

13. volatile: changeable, difficult to fix permanently.

13. intestine: the lower part of the alimentary canal, hence bowels.

THE MARVEL

2. spreadeagled: stretched out in the form of a spread eagle.

9. enlarging glass: a magnifying glass.

SIMPLIFY ME WHEN I'M DEAD

18. wrong-way telescope: a telescope is an optical instrument for enlarging the image of a distant object, so that a 'wrong-way telescope' would have the opposite effect of reducing the image.

21. lens: the glass part of the telescope through which the rays of light pass.

EGYPTIAN SENTRY, CORNICHE, ALEXANDRIA

8. rifle-muzzle: the end of the rifle from which the shot is fired.

10. tarbush: derived from 'tarboosh'—a brimless, usually red, felt cap worn by Mohammedans. Since the soldier is in khaki uniform the cap is khaki in this case.

14. *millionaire of smells:* a millionaire is one whose posses-
sions can be valued at a million or more; hence to be a
'millionaire of smells' one would be surrounded by
innumerable smells.

24. *shut out the moon with slats:* to close the slatted
shutters.

BEHAVIOUR OF FISH IN AN EGYPTIAN TEA
GARDEN

6–7. *submarine fronds:* underwater ferns.

8. *carmined:* finger nails painted crimson.

9. *cotton magnate:* a person of some importance or
power in the cotton industry.

13. *crustacean:* having a crustlike shell, like a crab.

CAIRO JAG

4. *levitation:* the illusion of suspending the human body
in the air without support.

7. *Décédé:* deceased.

8. *jasmin:* ornamental plant with fragrant, usually
white, flowers.

13. *hashish:* an intoxicating preparation, from Indian
hemp, for smoking.

16. *Holbein:* a great German painter who specialized
in portraits of notable personages.

21. *somnambulists:* sleep-walkers.

26. *metal brambles:* barbed wire.

VERGISSMEINICHT. German for 'forget-me-not'.

2. *nightmare ground:* the battlefield.

9. *gunpit spoil:* after a battle in previous centuries it was
a custom on the part of some survivors to collect what
was of value from the corpses. Here the word 'spoil' is
used with irony since all that the dead soldier had was
a stained and faded photograph of his girl friend.

12. *gothic script:* The Goths were an early German race.
In England, the type used for printing German, as
distinct from roman and italic characters, is called
'Gothic'. All the strokes of such a script have a uniform
width.

164

18. swart flies: black flies, with the implication that they are in some sense malignant.

3. the stars will not put down a hand: the stars are remote and indifferent.

6. cruel tracts of space: 'cruel' because the elements have no sympathy for the soldier-poet in his loneliness and misery. Later in the poem Douglas likens his lover to the indifferent elements.

20. swarthy: having a dark hue or cast. Douglas catches the tone of folk-song in the preceding three lines and thus links his personal feelings with countless others in the past.

HOW TO KILL

1. parabola: a geometrical term—the locus of a point whose distance from the focus is equal to its distance from a given straight line. Here the term is being used generally in reference to a ball thrown in the air; but since a 'parabole' is a comparison, a double meaning may be intended.

7. dial of glass: the sights of a machine-gun.

11. wires touch his face: as the sights of the gun are centred on the man, the intersecting wires appear to touch the face of the prospective target.

12. familiar: a member of the family or a close friend; in another sense, a spirit supposed to attend upon and obey a sorcerer.

ENFIDAVILLE

1. fallen like dancers: the church has collapsed as a result of bombardment.

2. the Virgin and St Thérèse: images of the Virgin Mary and St Thérèse.

ARISTOCRATS. 'I think I am becoming a God'—from the words the Roman Emperor, Nero, on his deathbed.

1. The noble horse: a satirical metaphor for the stiff-lipped, clean-living, pipe-smoking, Englishman of the upper-middle class, equating the fox-hunting rider with his horse.

3. *the shires:* a term applied to those counties of England the names of which end in -shire, with the added implication of the countryside and fox-hunting country.

10. *obsolescent:* out of date.

11. *unicorns:* legendary animals supposed to have a horse's body and a single horn in its forehead, thought to be a very trusting sort of creature, to be captured by guile; the representations of these animals are used a great deal in coats of arms, hence 'stupidity and chivalry'.

15. *cricket pitch:* a reference to the love of cricket of the type of Englishman portrayed, satirising the saying that the 'battle of Waterloo was won on the playing fields of Eton'.

16. *drop fences:* refers to the fox-hunting inclinations of the type portrayed.

20. *hunting horn:* a horn on which signals are blown in fox-hunting.

ON A RETURN FROM EGYPT

4. *sloe-eyed:* the sloe is the black or dark-purple fruit of the blackthorn.

5. *exquisites:* those who excite admiration—usually for their attention to dress or manners.

5. *under a curse:* destined, as victim, to some evil or disaster.

8. *cerulean:* blue or azure.

Sidney Keyes

From *The Collected Poems of Sidney Keyes* (1945)

ADVICE FOR A JOURNEY

9. *So take no rations:* during wartime certain foods were rationed to the whole population owing to the shortage,

21. *The fifes cry death:* the fife is a musical instrument, used mainly to accompany the drum by military bands.

25. *the raven is no sibyl:* both images are from mythology—the raven appears largely as a bird of omen, the sibyl was one of several women who predicted the future

under the inspiration of a particular deity in ancient Greece. Keyes appears to be urging his generation to face the idea of death—there is, he implies here, no uncertainty about the future and nothing to be gained by clinging to illusions about it.

28. Canaan: the ancient name of western Palestine, the promised land of the Jews after their journey through the wilderness.

EUROPE'S PRISONERS

3. arclights: extremely powerful electric lights which were shone in the faces of prisoners under interrogation in the European prison camps.

5. citizens of time: subject to time and hence here for a short time only.

19. Dachau: one of the most notorious prison camps of the Nazis, and reputed to be one of the most difficult from which to escape.

TROLL KINGS. From Scandinavian mythology, a race of supernatural beings originally conceived as giants, hence they are 'big-boned'; but Keyes has extended the meaning to include figures from British legend (King Arthur, etc) as well as such historical characters as Attila and Alexander. According to Scandinavian *Eddas*, there would come a time when, after a tremendous battle (Ragnorok) in which the gods themselves would be involved, the whole earth, together with its inhabitants and gods, would finally be destroyed; then a new heaven and earth would arise out of the sea. Clearly, this is the intended reference here since the troll kings await 'the time of terror' (l. 4).

3. with drawn-up knees: a reference to the ancient practice of burying distinguished persons with the knees drawn up.

6. Seraphion: From Greek myth; Perseus turned the inhabitants of Seriphus into stone with the head of the Gorgon.

7. lacunae: empty space or cavity.

8. *Arthur:* central figure of the Arthurian Saga in British legend, though there is some historical basis for the belief that he was a local chieftain who lived in the fifth or sixth century. There are many conflicting accounts of King Arthur, but perhaps the best known is that recorded by Malory in *Morte d'Arthur*, which features the adventures of Arthur's knights of the Round Table, the quest of the Holy Grail, and the guilty love of Launcelot for Queen Guenevere, wife of Arthur.

11. *Avalon:* in Arthurian legend, the land of the dead, to which Arthur was mysteriously borne after his death in battle.

12. *Lancelot too, the double lover:* the most famous of Arthur's knights. According to legend, Launcelot was the lover not only of Queen Guenevere, but also of Elaine, the 'Fair Maid of Astolat', though in Malory's account Launcelot, under a spell, supposes Elaine to be Guenevere.

15–16. *the guessed-at Grail:* In medieval legend, the Holy Grail was the vessel in which Christ's blood was received by Joseph of Arimathea at the crucifixion. The quest of the Holy Grail was undertaken by several knights of the Round Table, but it could be achieved only by the knight who was 'clean of sin'; hence for Launcelot, burdened by his guilty love, it is 'guessed-at'.

17. *Ragnar:* see note to title. Ragnar is the central figure of an old Icelandic poem, *The Death-Song of Ragner Lodbrog.*

25. *Barbarossa:* another name for Frederick I of Germany, who died during the Third Crusade; according to legend he sleeps in a cave in the Kyffhäuser mountain, surrounded by his companions.

26. *Attila:* as king of the Huns, ravaged and plundered eastern Europe during the fifth century.

28. *Alexander:* Alexander the Great, king of Macedon, who united all Greece and conquered a large part of Asia.

THE EXPECTED GUEST. The Guest is the dying god, both Christ and Adonis.

8. *the beast in the myrtle wood:* Adonis was killed by a wild boar.

10. *Veronica:* the woman who, according to legend, met Christ on the way to Calvary and wiped his face with her kerchief ('her flaxen cloth as yet unsigned'), which afterwards miraculously retained the imprint of Christ's features.

THE WILDERNESS. Written shortly before Keyes's death in 1943. The first canto of George Darley's *Nepenthe* formed the starting-point of the poem, which was originally dedicated 'I. M. Geoffrey Chaucer, George Darley, T. S. Eliot, the other explorers'.

22. *Longinus:* Greek philosopher of the third century A.D.

Guillaume de Lorris: French author of the first part of an allegorical love poem, *Roman de la Rose,* written in the thirteenth century.

39. *the metal bird sings madly from the fire:* the phoenix, a sacred bird of magnificent plumage, fabled to appear every 500 years out of the Arabian desert, when it burned itself on a funeral pile, and rose again young and beautiful, from its own ashes; hence a symbol of resurrection.

78. *Solomon Eagle:* a Quaker who appeared as a prophet during the Great Plague of London, calling upon the city to repent.

Three months after completing this poem, Keyes was killed on the Tunisian front.

Henry Reed

From *A Map of Verona* (1946)

THE DOOR AND THE WINDOW

2. *mystery:* the poet makes no attempt to define the mystery—the strange feeling he experiences on

waking in the early morning darkness—except to say that it was an intense feeling of isolation; he was unable to recognise the room and his distress was increased by the supposed absence of his lover.

LIVES

2. *wire a summer's roses:* florists wire the flowers to hold them together in the desired arrangement when making up bouquets.

8. *domicile:* to provide with a home or place of residence; the meaning here has been extended to include a prisoner-of-war camp.

13. *recalcitrant:* rebellious, not complying.

14. *remonstrances:* appeals or reproofs.

NAMING OF PARTS. This poem, together with 'Judging Distances' and 'Unarmed Combat', makes up a sequence entitled 'Lessons of the War', dealing with the procedures and conventions of army training.

1. *Naming of parts:* The army instructor is teaching the recruits the names and functions of different parts of the rifle. There are, in fact, two voices throughout the poem, that of the instructor using the army idiom, and that of the poet-commentator, mockingly using the same phrases, but giving them a more human meaning to emphasise the conflict between the two aspects.

4. *Japonica:* a flowering shrub.

7–9. The lower sling swivel, upper sling swivel, piling swivel, safety catch, breech, bolt, and cocking piece, are all parts of the rifle.

24. *easing the spring:* there is a deliberate pun here which adds to the effect. By sliding the bolt we can ease the spring of the rifle; the bees, performing their natural function, can be said to be easing the season of Spring.

JUDGING DISTANCES. As in the previous poem, there is great play upon words used in army training—judging the distance, the central sector, the right of arc, left of arc, etc. In this poem the soldiers are being

trained how to make an official report on an observed
landscape.

42. about one year and a half: another play upon words—
the soldier poet is separated from the observed lovers
because it is eighteen months since he had the same
freedom of action as the lovers, and he also judges
them to be about a year and a half younger (or they,
too, might be in the Forces).

UNARMED COMBAT

9. coin a phrase: to invent a phrase, employed satiric-
ally here since it is so obviously part of a well-used
army idiom.

21. Jerry: slang for German soldier.

SOUTH. This is the third poem of a sequence entitled
'The Desert', though it stands as a separate poem.

3. blizzard centre: a blizzard is a furious blast of cold wind
and blinding snow. Used in the context of the poem it
would imply that the protagonists have been drawn to
the stormy centre of the 'suffering god'.

42. calve: there are two meanings to the verb 'calve'—to
give birth and, of a glacier, to throw off a mass of ice.
Though the latter is obviously intended here and is
more relevant to the line, there is an implied sense of
the former.

43. tack: in the nautical sense, to make a run or course
obliquely against the wind, which may involve con-
stant changes of direction; a kind of zigzag course.

45. recondite: hidden from sight or understanding.

ISEULT LA BELLE. Ostensibly concerned with the
legend of Tristram and Iseult, this poem uses the
legend to explore its implications for mankind. In
the legend Tristram falls in love with Iseult though
she is destined to marry King Mark of Cornwall,
and becomes the Queen. The love between Tristram
and Iseult continues after her marriage to Mark until
Tristram is finally banished. After a series of adven-
tures at King Arthur's court, and in Brittany, Tristram
marries another Iseult (Blaunchesmains) though he

never forgets the first Iseult. There are various endings
to the story, but in some of them Tristram returns
to Cornwall and scales the castle-wall to see his
original love.

59. chimerical: imaginary or visionary.

Roy Fuller

From *The Middle of a War* (1942)

SOLILOQUY IN AN AIR RAID

2. formication: an itching sensation, as if a small insect
was creeping over the skin.

5. phthisic: asthmatic.

16. epicentrum: the point over the centre; in seismology the
point of outbreak of earthquake shocks.

27. Jonson: Ben Jonson (1572–1637). In *The Staple of
News*, Jonson satirized both the credulity of the age
and the abuse of riches.
bourgeoisie: the middle class.

38. Kerensky: Russian Socialist Minister of Justice and,
later, of War, in the Provisional Government follow-
ing the Revolution of March 1917. He was removed
by the Military Committee, in November 1917.
Lenin: One of the most prominent leaders of the Rus-
sian Revolution, leader of the Bolsheviki. President
of the Council of the Russian Republic.

46. the Hundred Years' War: Between England and
France, 1337–1453.

EPITAPH ON A BOMBING VICTIM

8. confederate: ally of, or in league with, History.

THE MIDDLE OF A WAR

2. the matelot's collar: matelot = sailor (Fuller served in
the Royal Navy during the war). The collar of the Bri-
tish sailor's uniform had three white rings, tradition-
ally celebrating Nelson's three great naval victories.

12. Life has been abandoned by the boats: when a ship is
sinking the crew take to the boats and abandon ship.

Y.M.C.A. WRITING ROOM. During wartime the

Young Men's Christian Association provided residential and other facilities for men on leave from the Forces.

4. *dangerous blues and reds:* on the maps in use at the time the sea was indicated in blue and components of the British Empire in red.

5. *drafted:* earmarked for service with the Army, Navy or Air Force.

20. *the sacred wood:* See *The Golden Bough* by James Fraser. In antiquity the grove sacred to Diana ('the sacred wood') was the place where the priest-king (or sacrificial victim) was slain by his successor as king of the wood. The ordeal of walking in the sacred wood was that one might be set upon and slain at any moment.

HARBOUR FERRY. In this poem Fuller despondently contemplates the complete destruction of mankind and a future of earth in which man has no part.

From *A Lost Season* (1944)

IN AFRICA. Fuller was stationed in East Africa for a time. In this poem he attempts to equate his own feelings of loneliness and exile with the hills and the existence of the hunted lions ('made shabby with rifles').

THE GREEN HILLS OF AFRICA

14. *the wicked habit:* There is a pun here—the village wears the corrugated iron like a habit (garment) and the store itself is the centre for practices (habits) which might be deplored.

THE GIRAFFES

17. *bovine:* sluggish.

THE PLAINS

18. *The headlights:* the giraffes at night are being observed from motor vehicles.

32. *archetypal:* primitive or original.

DURING A BOMBARDMENT BY V-WEAPONS. V weapons were the flying bombs (V1s) and rockets (V2s) which the Germans invented and put into use against England towards the end of the war and with which they hoped to turn the tide.

Edith Sitwell

From *Street Songs* (1942)

Edith Sitwell's world of imagination has its own set of constants, basic images which are used again and again—the Lion, the Nails of the Cross, the Skeleton, the Rose, the Bone, the Sun, Ixion's Wheel, golden things (i.e. armour, corn, etc.) and green things which have freshness and life—but in her later years these were presented in new patterns of experience or explored at greater depth. Unfortunately, as Sir Kenneth Clark remarked in his obituary article, 'she felt that the mere repetition of these words was enough to produce the effect of poetry, and she became so obsessed with them that certain combinations of magic-making words reappear in almost identical form in several of her late poems'.

STILL FALLS THE RAIN

1. the Rain: Edith Sitwell had previously made use of the 'rain' image in a somewhat superficial manner; here she gives the image tremendous impact by relating it to the falling of bombs on the cities in a sinister rain during the raids of 1940, hence the 'rain' is black.

3. blind: blind in its destructive action and in such shortsighted vision as that responsible for the crucifixion, indeed, the continuing crucifixion—for the poem suggests that even in 1940 mankind is still driving the nails into Christ's hands and feet: 'blind as the nineteen hundred and forty nails'. The parallel with the crucifixion establishes the deeply religious note of the poem.

7. Potter's Field: see Matthew, 27:7.

The name given to a piece of land to provide a burial ground for the poor and strangers, purchased with the thirty pieces of silver Judas threw down in the temple after the betrayal of Christ, 'wherefore that field was called the Field of Blood'.

9. Field of Blood: see comment above.

10. Cain: according to Genesis, the first murderer.

12. Starved Man: Christ.

14. Dives and Lazarus: see the parable of Lazarus (Luke 16). 'Dives' is a latin word meaning 'rich man'. In the parable Lazarus was a beggar, so the implication of the line is that the Rain falls on rich and poor, guilty and innocent, alike.

17. the Blood: the Rain can also be regarded as the blood flowing from the wounded side of the crucified Christ and, therefore, holds promise of redemption, even for those who inflicted, and those who are still inflicting, the wounds.

25. O Ile leap up to my God, who pulles me doune—
See, see where Christ's blood streames in the firmament;
Taken from Marlowe's *Doctor Faustus* (from the last soliloquy of Faustus who, having previously sold his soul to the Devil, desperately tries to avert his punishment in Hell).

30. Caesar's laurel crown: the crown of thorns placed upon the head of Christ by the roman soldiers.

LULLABY

3. steel birds': the raiding bombers overhead.

5. out danced the Babioun: the phrase is taken from an epigram by Ben Jonson. Here the image of a monstrous ape acting as fostermother to the war-orphaned child is intended to reflect the human situation during the destructive years of the war.

10. do, do, do, do: the refrain of the lullaby sung by the Babioun.

12. the Pterodactyl: a winged reptile, now extinct. In keeping with the mood of the poem, the bombing plane is equated with the pterodactyl; it lays a steel egg in the earth and 'fouls its nest'.

14. Judas-coloured: betraying.

25. Poland, Spain: the reference is to the bombing of cities in the invasion of Poland during the Second

World War, and of Spain in the Spanish Civil War.

SERENADE: ANY MAN TO ANY WOMAN. In this poem Edith Sitwell makes use of echoes from Elizabethan love-songs in order to present contrast.

7. *unfaithful I, the cannon's mate:* since the young man will inevitably be killed, he is by implication 'the cannon's mate', and hence unfaithful to his love.

13. *lies shall be your canopy:* as the destined victim of war cannot be true to his love, and is aware of his position, he is unable to keep any of his promises.

21. *Then die with me and be my love:* Marlowe's 'Then live with me and be my love', from 'The Passionate Shepherd', inverted to point the irony.

From *Green Song* (1944)

A MOTHER TO HER DEAD CHILD

43. *pruriency of the Ape:* the recurring image of the Ape; see 'Lullaby' for the Babioun, with whom this image is connected.

HEART AND MIND

14. *Hercules:* from Greek mythology, the son of Zeus and Alcmena, noted for his tremendous strength.

15. *Samson:* from the Old Testament, also noted for his strength.
pillars of the seas: the mountains facing one another at the entrance to the Mediterranean Sea are called the Pillars of Hercules, since according to legend they were parted by Hercules.

From *The Canticle of the Rose* (1949)

DIRGE FOR THE NEW SUNRISE

1. *Ixion to the wheel:* one of Edith Sitwell's recurring images. According to Greek mythology, Zeus banished Ixion to hell and decreed that he should be tied to a perpetually revolving wheel.

7. *Nero:* Roman emperor (A.D. 37–68), proverbial for his brutality, particularly to Christians.

15. zircon: a native silicate of zirconium, occurring in tetragonal crystals of various colours, some of which are used as gems.

20. mammoth: large extinct species of elephant formerly native in Europe and Asia.

31. Megatherium Mylodon: extinct species of giant sloth.

32. Mastodon: large extinct mammal resembling the elephant.

73. monstrous bull-voices of unseen fearful mimes: a fragment taken from the lost play by Aeschylus, *The Edonians.*

77. the Son of God is sowed in every furrow: John Donne, *Sermon XI.*

78. the Cloud in the Heavens: the exploding atomic bomb at Hiroshima.

83. transcript of an actual report by an eye-witness of the dropping of the bomb.

97–99. Founded on a passage in Burnet's *Theory of the Earth.*

116–120. These are references to descriptions given by Lombroso and Havelock Ellis of the marks and appearance borne by prenatally disposed criminals.

119. lemurine: of the lemur genus; an animal allied to the monkey but having a pointed muzzle.

129–130. Paracelsus, Appendix 1, ch. vi:- 'Also we must say that this or that is a disease of Gold, and not that it is leprosy.'

139–148. These verses contain references to Hermetic writings (relating to occult sciences, especially alchemy).

159–160. John Donne, *Sermon CXXXVI.*

THE CANTICLE OF THE ROSE

4. almandine: an alumina iron garnet of violet or amethystine tint.

30–32. Transcript of an eye-witness's description of Nagasaki after the falling of the atomic bomb.

59. Anturs of Arthur, 1394.

60. Wyclif, *Selected Writings.*

Edwin Muir

From *The Narrow Place* (1943)

THE NARROW PLACE

3. javelin: a short, light spear.

THE GOOD MAN IN HELL

10. rescindless: not to be annulled or taken away.

11. rote: repetition of words with little attention to sense.

13. station: his assigned location.

18. Eden: the Garden of Eden, the first abode of Adam and Eve; but used by Muir as an archetypal symbol for a return to man's lost innocence.

From *The Voyage* (1946)

THE CASTLE

2. turret: a small tower rising above the wall of the castle.

7. provender: food.

8. battlements: the parapets along the top of the castle walls, usually indented on their upper line to permit the defenders to aim their weapons at the attackers.

14. dead or quick: dead or alive.

19. wicket gate: a small gate subsidiary to, or made within, a larger entrance.

20. wizened: withered or shrunken.

MOSES. Lawgiver and leader of the Israelites, who led his people out of captivity in Egypt.

1. Pisgah: the mountain east of Jordan from which Moses was allowed a view of the Promised Land of Canaan (now Israel).

2. holiday land: The Promised Land of the Jews, frequently referred to in the Bible as the 'land flowing with milk and honey'. The seventh day of the week (the Sabbath) is the day of rest and worship for the Jews (Israelis) as enjoined upon them by the fourth commandment of the Decalogue; hence Canaan was both a 'holiday' land and a sabbath land for the returning Jews, coming from slavery and oppression in Egypt.

3. *prophetic beasts:* Since the Lord had promised to give Canaan to the Israelites, and to help them drive out the occupying peoples, the flocks and herds of the latter would pass into the hands of the invaders as spoils of war; the sight of these beasts reminded Moses of the divine promise, hence they were in a sense 'prophetic'.

4. *lintel:* a horizontal piece of timber (or stone) placed over an entrance or opening in the wall to bear the weight of the structure above the opening.

18. *aboriginal:* the first or earliest known; pertaining to the indigenous peoples of Canaan.

23. *diaspora:* the dispersion of the Jewish race (first mentioned as a warning in the Bible, Deuteronomy 28:25).

26. *offal:* refuse or waste.

27. *ghetto:* the quarter in a city to which the Jews were restricted. Although Toledo, Cracow, Vienna and Budapest are specifically listed, the reference is to the oppression of the Jews, not merely in Spain, Poland, Austria and Hungary, but throughout Europe.

38. *migrations:* movements of races or peoples from one country to another.

40. *Jordan:* the river Jordan in Israel.

From *The Labyrinth* (1949)

THE LABYRINTH

1. *labyrinth:* an intricate structure of communicating passages through which it is difficult to find one's way. The reference here is to the legendary labyrinth constructed for Minos, King of Crete. According to legend, after defeating the Athenians, Minos demanded a yearly tribute of seven youths and seven maidens to be brought to the Labyrinth at Crete, where they were devoured by the Minotaur (half bull, half man), until Theseus destroyed the monster. However, Muir

179

is using the theme to illustrate his own experience; his life in Glasgow and his later conflicts of mind.

4. *I'd meet myself returning:* an attempt to describe his own conflicting and contradictory states of mind (he was like 'a spirit seeking his body').

11. *Hades:* in Greek legend, the lower world or place of departed spirits after life on earth.

20–23. *the maze itself . . . :* Muir tells us elsewhere that his experience of life was that of being in a maze until the time of his marriage, when his eyes were opened to 'the lovely world'.

69. *embowered:* enclosed.

THE CHILD DYING

16. *phantom:* something that has only an apparent existence.

THE COMBAT

2. *that combat:* the continual struggle between good and evil.

THE INTERROGATION. In this poem Muir is making use of his experience of those European countries in which a person could be called upon at any hour of the day or night to be questioned and perhaps tortured in an attempt to secure information.

THE GOOD TOWN. Although Muir records the Communist takeover of Prague in 1948, he is using the event as an illustration of the way in which good is betrayed by evil, from within (see also 'The Castle').

5. *antiquities:* relics of an earlier time.

6. *gyves:* shackles or fetters.

18. *sojourners:* temporary guests or residents.

71. *informers:* those who make it their business to detect offenders against laws and regulations and to inform the authorities.

SOLILOQUY

31. *Platonic:* relevant to the doctrines of the Greek philosopher, Plato; love that is purely spiritual rather than physical.

35. *watershed:* the line separating the waters flowing into different rivers.

47. *Troy:* according to legend, as related by Homer in the *Iliad*, Troy was the capital of King Priam and was for ten years besieged by the Greeks. The city is reputed to have stood near the Hellespont and the river Scamander in Asia Minor.

56. *anthology:* a collection.

92. *Sol:* the sun.

94. *Systole and diastole:* the regular contraction of the heart that drives the blood outward and the relaxation of the heart in rhythmic alternation.

THE TRANSFIGURATION. In this poem Muir presents his conception of the experience recorded in Matthew 17, when Jesus took three of his disciples, Peter, James and John, up a high mountain—'And was transfigured before them: and his face did shine as the sun, and his raiment was white as the light'.

17. *Eden:* the garden of Eden, symbol of man's lost innocence.

29. *the starting-day:* the first day of creation.

50. *he will come again:* a reference to the belief, held by Christians, that Christ will make a second coming.

Vernon Watkins

From *The Ballad of the Mari Lwyd* (1941)

THE COLLIER

1. *When I was born . . . :* the speaker is the survivor of a pit disaster. Amman hill is in Wales.

21. *A coloured coat:* the young man is symbolically identified with Joseph of the Biblical story (Genesis 37), Joseph was given a coat of many colours; out of jealousy, his brothers thrust him down a pit, prior to selling him to the passing Midianites. By this means, Watkins connects a legend with reality.

25. *They dipped my coat:* The poem follows the biblical story to some extent. Joseph's coat was dipped in the blood of a kid so that his brothers could convince

their father that he had been attacked by a savage beast.

35. interpreted their dreams: Joseph had his own dreams which he interpreted to the annoyance of his brothers.

37. leper's lamp: Miner's lamp.

39. after-damp: the choke-damp left in a coal mine after an explosion.

From *The Lady With the Unicorn* (1948)

SARDINE-FISHERS AT DAYBREAK

7. Milky Way: a luminous band encircling the heavens, composed of distant stars and nebulae invisible separately to the human eye.

31. octopus-dark: the eight-armed (or tentacled) octopus tends to lurk in dark caverns or crevices in the sea-bed.

32. tunnies: one of the largest of food-fish; has been fished in the Mediterranean and Atlantic from ancient times.

35. cairn: a pyramid of rough stones raised in earlier times in honour of the dead.

41. dinghy: small rowing boat.

58. winding-sheets: sheets in which corpses are wrapped for burial.

89. caul: the membrane enclosing the foetus before birth; it is regarded as lucky if the child is born with part of the caul enveloping the head.

THE FEATHER

6. horny quill: the tube or stem of a feather, the part by which it is attached to the skin.

31. the Furies: from Greek myth; the avenging deities who executed the curses pronounced upon criminals, or inflicted famine and pestilence. The Furies also spun the thread of human destiny. The name Eumenides ('the kindly ones') was also given to them in the hope of appeasing them and averting their anger.

THE HEALING OF THE LEPER. This poem takes as its subject the healing of the leper recorded in various parts of the New Testament (Matthew 8, Mark 1, Luke 5, and other places), though it is possible that

Watkins took the incident from Mark ch. 3, where it
is recorded that the Pharisees were watching Jesus
to see if He would heal the leper on the Sabbath
day. Before healing the man, Jesus turned to the
Pharisees and said: 'Is it lawful to do good on the
sabbath day, or to do evil? to save life, or to kill?'

5. *which time interred:* although the leper was cured,
the 'withered hand' is interred (buried) by time in
two senses; first, it was in the time of his past exper-
ience that the victim contracted leprosy; second,
since the healing of the withered hand is recorded
in the Bible, for all time, it is continually being
interred.

9. *Plotinus:* Born in Egypt, Plotinus was the founder of
the neo-Platonic Philosophy. Since he developed
Plato's teaching (of spiritual love), he might be said
to have preached on 'heaven's floor'; that is, he
preached the kind of love which is the basis of
Christianity.

13. *Botticelli:* Botticelli was a Florentine painter (1447–
1510) who sought inspiration in the works of Dante
and Boccaccio. A religious painter, Botticelli is noted
for the undulating character of line (he has been called
the 'greatest poet of line'), but Watkins may also be
referring to his plastic form, his sense of beauty and
grace, his apparent hesitation between two worlds
(pagan and Christian), or his form, colour and
composition.

LACE-MAKER

2. *Samothrace:* an island in the Aegean Sea, whose
inhabitants initiated the Samothracian mysteries
(religious rites).

5. *your untranslatable love:* Watkins is not merely de-
scribing the lace-maker, but using images from lace-
making as symbols for a deeper meaning.

14. *bobbins:* small wooden pins, with a notch, used in
lace-making.

42. *to fast:* to abstain from food as a deliberate relig-

ious observance. Here the term is appropriate since, instead of selling the results of her labour and thereby obtaining money for food, the old lace-maker has chosen to make a gift of the lace to the church.

THE BUTTERFLIES

30. weir: an obstruction placed in a stream to raise the water in order to divert it into a mill-race or irrigation ditch.

36. fosse: a canal, ditch or trench.

ZACCHEUS IN THE LEAVES. Another poem based upon an episode recorded in the Bible, in which the biblical event is brought into relation with the human situation. The biblical story is taken from Luke 19, which records how a publican called Zaccheus, a small man unable to see Jesus because of the crowds, climbed a tree to get a glimpse of Jesus as He passed. As a result Zaccheus was converted.

8. the myth above the myth: The myth of Christ over that of the Tree of Life (for Watkins is equating the sycamore tree with the World Tree of mythology).

15. Dionysiac: relating to the Greek god, Dionysus (or his Roman equivalent, Bacchus) god of wine, representing the power of wine.

16. Pan's music: Pan was the god of the fields, of flocks and shepherds, reported to have made a reed instrument called the syrinx on which he played rustic melodies.

41. Sibyl: a woman who predicted the future; presumably the implication here is that Zaccheus's future was predicted when he climbed the tree.

43. Sibylline words: thuse uttered or written by the Sibyl (see above).

107. the Muses: the nine sister-goddesses regarded as the inspiration of learning and the arts, especially of music and poetry.

Dylan Thomas

From *Deaths and Entrances* (1946)

THE CONVERSATION OF PRAYER. Note particularly the intricate rhyming pattern with its hidden rhyme in the middle of each line which, together with the vowel music, gives the poem its incantatory effect. Observe, too, how Thomas achieves the counterpoint of the poem with its two themes of the man and the child, like two distinct melodies, curiously interwoven and interdependent. This is a paradoxical poem in which two kinds of prayer are contrasted.

11. same grief flying: both prayers are motivated by the same human hopes and fears.

14. turns on the quick and the dead: there may be a triple meaning here: first, that the prayer affects both the living and the dead; second, that one prayer is answered (quick = living) whilst the other is not; and third, that the power of the child's prayer is *turned* (transferred) upon the object of the man's deep concern.

18. shall drown in a grief as deep as his true grave: the poem implies that the grief of the man is transferred to the child. It should be remembered that many people still believe in the transferability of the grace acquired through genuine prayer—that prayer accumulates as a kind of vast reserve upon which all may draw, so that the prayers of the innocent benefit other people.

A REFUSAL TO MOURN THE DEATH, BY FIRE, OF A CHILD IN LONDON.
Although Thomas was not a 'war poet', this poem, about a child killed in an air-raid during the war, is perhaps one of the most memorable poems of the war-time period.

1–6. The child's death is seen against the background of the whole of creation from beginning to the end.

6. *sea tumbling in harness:* the action of waves breaking on the shore, controlled by tidal laws (i.e. 'in harness').

7–9. A reference to his own death, when his body will merge with the common elements of the earth (the 'waterbead' and 'ear of corn').

12. *in the least valley of sackcloth:* a derivation from the biblical phrase 'in sackcloth and ashes'—sackcloth was worn and ashes sprinkled on the head as a sign of lamentation. The poet vows not to mourn the death of the child until he, too, must die.

14–15. *I shall not murder/ The mankind of her going:* the poet refuses to make a conventional display of grief since this would be a betrayal of the child's humanity.

16. *stations of the breath:* a derivation from 'Stations of the Cross', a series of pictures representing successive incidents in the Passion of Christ, usually found in Catholic churches.

24. *After the first death, there is no other:* An ambiguous line which can be construed in different ways. Professor Empson has interpreted it as an expression of 'pantheistic pessimism'; but it can equally well express the orthodox Christian belief of life after death—after the body is dead, the spirit lives for ever and there will be no more death. In view of Thomas's profession of belief in God (in the introduction to his *Collected Poems*) and his frequent references to the Resurrection in his later poems, it is contended that the second interpretation is more likely to be correct.

POEM IN OCTOBER

1. *thirtieth year to heaven:* the poem celebrates Thomas's thirtieth birthday.

12. *birds of the winged trees flying my name:* an example of Thomas's use of the transferred epithet or attribute. Here Thomas transfers the adjective 'winged' from birds to trees, since the trees are alive with birds and appear to be taking part in the celebration of his birthday; hence they seem to be 'flying' his name, as

children wave flags to welcome the arrival of a distinguished person.

17. *high tide:* there is a suggestion here that not only is the sea at high tide in the harbour, but that, metaphorically speaking, the poet's emotional life is at high tide as he climbs a hill to look down on the scene.

38–40. *There could I marvel/My birthday away:* as the poet gazes down on the town and harbour, he imagines the effect of spring and summer and feels at harmony with life, so that he can revel in the scene before him.

40. *but the weather turned around:* his mood changes as he remembers his age and recalls the innocent and splendid days of childhood.

42. *down the other air and the blue altered sky:* as he contemplates his childhood and recreates the childlike vision, he sees everything in another light and in an entirely different atmosphere.

THIS SIDE OF THE TRUTH. Written for the poet's son, Llewelyn, when he was six years old.

3. *king of your blue eyes:* supreme in innocence.

5. *all is undone:* this phrase, together with the remainder of the first stanza, suggests that everything is predetermined before one acts or even thinks: 'Before you move to make/One gesture of the heart or head.'

13–14. *Good and bad, two ways/Of moving about your death:* What we describe as good and bad actions are two sides of the same coin, and merely present two aspects of man's brief progress from birth to death.

36. *Die in unjudging love:* all good or evil actions, like man himself, are shortlived and soon cancelled out in the universal mercy and love with which we merge at death.

TO OTHERS THAN YOU

2. *You with a bad coin in your socket:* There is a double meaning here. First, there is a reference to Gresham's Law of Currency that 'bad money drives out good money', that is, when debased and sound coins are in

circulation together, people will inevitably hoard the good currency and pass on the bad. Hence the 'friend with a bad coin' is one whose actions deny his friendship, for he will pass on the bad coin. Since we expect coins to be kept in a pocket, the deliberate use of the rhyming word 'socket' gives the line an additional meaning that a false friend is as dangerous as a coin might be in the socket of a fuse box.

17. While you displaced a truth in air: in the language of science, one substance displaces another, hence the lie displaces truth.

THE HUNCHBACK IN THE PARK

3. Propped between trees and water: so disreputable in appearance as to resemble a scarecrow or a guy.

11. Slept at night in a dog kennel: the tramp's sleeping quarters were no more comfortable than a kennel.

14. Like the water he sat down: Since he always came early to the park, the town boys who tormented him rarely saw him walking, but came across him sitting or lying down.

25. And the old dog sleeper: he slept in quarters to be described as a kennel, hence he becomes an 'old dog'.

28. Made the tigers jump out of their eyes: whilst playing, the boys pretended to be fierce.

31–32. Made all day until bell time/ A woman figure without fault: living in abject circumstances, harassed by the boys, the lonely disreputable old tramp still has his dreams, symbolised by the figure of a beautiful young woman. In a sense, this poem is about the triumph of the imagination.

A WINTER'S TALE. This narrative poem, which derives its subject (though not its treatment) from Shakespeare's play of the same name, is about the fulfilment of a wish by magical means; the wish in this case being granted, not by the fairy godmother or the genie of the lamp, but by a she bird 'rayed like a burning bride'. Although the poem has all the qualities of the fairy story, it can also be interpreted as a folk tale symbolising the rebirth of spring.

3. *floating fields:* seen through the falling snow, the fields appear to be floating.

5. *pale breath of cattle at the stealthy sail:* in the wintry atmosphere the cattle's breath steams.

11. *Once when the world turned old:* a variation of the fairy-tale opening 'once when the world was young', which Thomas has changed to his own purposes, since the world has turned old for the man without a lover.

13–14. *a man unrolled/ The scrolls of fire:* prayed ardently or expressed a burning need.

24. *gentle in their clogs:* the milkmaids tread warily through the snow (which has fallen from the sky).

48–49. *white/Inhuman cradle:* in the urgency of the man's prayer for an answer to his need for love, the surrounding snow of the landscape becomes the snow of his lost childhood, yet at the same time the symbol of the love he is seeking.

66–67. *It was a hand or sound . . . that glided the dark door wide:* the prayer was heard.

69. *she bird:*, possibly derived from Celtic myth. Certainly presented as a divine apparition or an annunciation.

98. *All night lost and long wading in the wake of the she bird:* the man follows the divine bird.

116. *The rite is shorn:* the spell is broken.

130. *And she rose with him flowering in her melting snow:* in the terms of the story, the man's wish is fulfilled; in terms of folk lore, spring is reborn.

IN MY CRAFT OR SULLEN ART

1. *sullen art:* in order to write, the poet must isolate himself from other people and be unsociable; it may also be a cause for bitterness that the sacrifice required is neither recognised nor rewarded.

14. *spindrift pages:* shortlived like blown spray.

FERN HILL

7. *And once below a time:* a departure from the fairy-tale

opening 'Once upon a time', appropriate in that it emphasises that the child is subject to time, 'below' time.

11. *About the happy yard:* transferred epithet; it is, of course, the child who is happy, but by transferring the quality of happiness the poet heightens the effect.

12. *In the sun that is young once only:* another example of transferred attribute, for it is the child who is young once only; this enables Thomas to transfer the golden quality of the sun to the child in 14.

14. *Golden in the mercy of his means:* transferred attribute (see above).

30. *it was Adam and maiden:* everything was so fresh and innocent that it was like the time of Adam and Eve in the garden of Eden.

33. *So it must have been after the birth of the simple light:* this line, and the three lines following, refer to the story of the Creation as told in the first chapter of Genesis—'And God saw that it was good'; so the spellbound horses of 'Fern Hill' appropriately walk 'on to the fields of praise'.

51. *And wake to the farm forever fled from the childless land:* the happy carefree days of childhood have gone for ever.

It may not be too irrelevant, nor too controversial in its implications, to suggest an affinity between Wordsworth and Dylan Thomas in their attitude to lost childhood. A comparison of Wordsworth's 'Ode on Intimations of Immortality' with Thomas's 'Fern Hill' shows certain similarities in form, content, treatment and imagery (note the similarity between Wordsworth's 'apparelled in celestial light' and Thomas's 'Down the rivers of the windfall light', and the connection between Wordsworth's 'Shades of the prison-house begin to close . . .' and Thomas's 'Time held me green and dying/Though I sang in my chains. . .').

Norman Nicholson

From *Five Rivers* (1944)

ROCKFERNS

1. spleenwort: one of the various ferns of the genus *Asplenium*, its green stem and leaves resembling zipfasteners.

8. spores: the reproductive body in flowerless plants.

14. buckler frond: leafy stem of the fern visualised as a green arm holding a small round shield (buckler).

15. calcined: changed by the action of heat into a friable powder.

22. Betelgeuse: a reddish star of the first magnitude in the constellation known as Orion.

WAITING FOR SPRING 1943

4. dyker: country craftsman whose task it is to make and maintain dykes (ditches).

7. lamb's-tails: the catkins of the hazel.

9. perimeter: outer boundary of any area or surface. It might be thought unnecessary to repeat the idea in the word 'fringe' that follows in the line.

19. morphia: from *morphine*, a drug contained in opium and used for alleviating pain.

26. atonement: the condition of being at one with others; in theological terms, reconciliation with God.

THE EVACUEES. At the beginning of the war, when intensive bombing raids and gas attacks were anticipated, many of the women and children were evacuated (taken out) from the larger cities to country districts where they were billeted upon the local inhabitants. This was a tremendous disruption of the lives of the evacuees; so much so, that some of them, unused to country villages, returned to their home towns, despite the danger.

8. the walls of Poland fell: the war started with Germany's invasion of Poland.

13. Northumbrian voices: the evacuees in this case were evidently from Newcastle or other towns on the coast of Northumberland.

18. *Tyneside:* Newcastle upon Tyne, an important coal-mining area.

20. *Cumberland vowels:* the dialect of the places in Cumberland to which they were evacuated.

22. *aisle:* the part of a church on either side of the nave, or a passage between the rows of pews.

From *Rock Face* (1948)

NAAMAN. The poem retells the biblical story of Naaman the leper (2 Kings 5) 'captain of the host of the King of Syria', who, though an unbeliever, was cured of leprosy by God, working through the prophet Elisha. It is in fact the story of a conversion. As in his verse drama, Nicholson provides a modern Cumberland setting for the scene and uses a colloquial language.

8. *ragwort:* a herb of the genus *Senecio*, a tall smooth cottony plant with bright yellow flowers.

9. *This is the river:* in the biblical story, the river was the Jordan.

13. *scree:* a stony slope of broken stones upon a mountain side.

16. *The old man:* Elisha, the prophet.

17. *Wash my hands:* the actual biblical instruction was: 'Go and wash in Jordan seven times, and thy flesh shall come again to thee, and thou be clean.'

21. *pestle:* an instrument, usually club-shaped, for pounding substances in a bowl of hard material.

22. *spliced:* to splice is to unite (two parts of the same rope) by interweaving the strands of one end with that of the other; hence the implication here is that he would have wrinkled his forehead in intense prayer.

24. *tap:* obviously in Naaman's time there were no taps as part of a plumbing system. Nicholson has modernised the setting in order to stress the present day significance of the biblical episode and to make the story more realistic for modern readers.

TO A CHILD BEFORE BIRTH

2. *strident:* actually means making a loud noise, but

Nicholson is using the word to suggest that the skies are of such intense blue that they almost shout.

4. *fluke:* the word has several meanings, but the meaning intended here is that of an unexpected success or a lucky chance.

5. *you do not hear:* the thoughts are being expressed by a happy pregnant woman in relation to her unborn child.

8. *haws:* fruit of the hawthorn.

11. *throstles:* thrushes.

12. *may:* blossom of the hawthorn, so called because the tree blooms in May.

ACROSS THE ESTUARY. Nicholson informs us that 'in the days when the estuaries of Morecambe Bay and South Cumberland were crossed regularly by travellers on foot and by coach, the guides marked the track by planting branches of broom in the sands. This was called "brogging the sands".' In addition to the actual details of the poem, there is an intended reference to the crossing of the Red Sea as a symbol of the death of the natural man which precedes spiritual rebirth.

2. *Branching up the channels:* the tidal currents in this area are still very treacherous.

10. *cormorants:* large and voracious seabirds, black in colour, which do resemble question-marks as they stand on the rocks.

14. *Brogs of broom:* branches of broom (see note above).

14. *curlew:* one of the long-legged wading birds with a long curved bill.

16. *Byzantine:* belonging to Byzantium or Constantinople—byzantine architecture makes special use of round arches, circles, and domes.

21. *squids of sand:* squids are a species of cephalopod, like cuttle-fish etc, characterised by tentacles. Nicholson obviously means that the clumps of sand wrap round his feet as if attached by the suckers of squid tentacles.

40. *quicksand:* a bed of extremely loose wet sand, easily

yielding to pressure and capable of swallowing a man or animal walking upon it. There are still quicksands in the area.

47. flabbergasting: utterly astonishing and confusing.

70. salvaging: saving.

81. sedge and plantain: coarse grasslike plants growing in wet places and herbs with broad flat leaves spread close to the ground.

86. calico: white cotton cloth, easily torn.
   sun lets down its ropes: the rays of sunshine break through the fog.

SILECROFT SHORE. One of the particular features of Norman Nicholson's work is his preoccupation with the creative and cyclic processes of life, expressed in terms of landscape and geology, as in this poem.

25. nap of turf: turf having a pile, or a surface given to cloth by artificial raising of the short fibres.
   nibs of marram: sea reed or bent grass with points like pen-nibs.

32. wrack: seaweed cast ashore.

34. barnacles: small shell-fish found attached to rocks, ships etc. Nicholson calls them 'little volcanoes' because of their shape.

35. Skiddaw or Black Combe: Skiddaw is a mountain in the Lake District which provides Skiddaw slate, a mud-rock; Black Combe is a fell on the coast which dominates the coast line from Lancashire to Scotland, and is the largest outcrop of Skiddaw slate in the south of Cumberland.

38. rhomboids: lozenge-shaped objects or formations.

61. gimlet: to make holes as with a gimlet (a small boring tool).

64. granophyr: igneous granite rock that has a ground-mass enclosing crystals of feldspar or quartz.
   shale: rock resembling slate.

65. stope: excavating tool used in mining.

69. solders: unites.

70. *savannahs:* tracks of level land covered with low vegetation.
73. *grottoes:* small caverns.
75. *ordovician:* pertaining to the series of Lower Silurian rocks.
86. *beck:* brook with a stony bed.
99. *stalactites:* icicle-like formations of calcium carbonate, depending from the roof of a cavern.
102. *arthritic:* the disease, arthritis, affects the joints; the word is used here to describe the distorted shape of the branches of the thorntrees.

Biographical and Bibliographical Notes

Alun Lewis

Born at Cwmaman, near Aberdare, Wales, in 1915 (d. 1944). Son of the Director of Education at Aberdare, he was educated at the University of Wales where he took a first in history in 1935. After two years' postgraduate research at Manchester University, had completed his O.C.T.U. course in the Lake District. Posted to teacher at Lewis's Secondary School, Pengarn. He was called up in 1940 and joined the 6th Battalion of the South Wales Borderers. He married Gweno Ellis in the following year, when he had completed his O.C.T.U. course in the Lake District. Posted to India in 1944, he was accidentally wounded by a pistol shot at Goppe Pass and died shortly afterwards in the casualty clearing station at Bawli. His publications include the following volumes, all published by Allen & Unwin:

Raiders' Dawn, 1942.
The Last Inspection, short stories, 1943.
Ha! Ha! Among the Trumpets, 1945.
Letters from India, selected by Gweno Lewis and Gwyn Jones, 1946.
Under the Green Tree, letters and short stories, 1948.

Keith Douglas

Born at Tunbridge Wells, Kent, in 1920 (d. 1943). He won scholarships to Christ's Hospital and then Merton College, Oxford, in October, 1938, where his tutor, Edmund Blunden, assisted him in getting his early poems published. Whilst at Oxford, he edited *Augury* for Blackwells, and *The Cherwell*. One of the eight poets represented in *Eight Oxford Poets* (Routledge). Although a member of Oxford O.T.C., he was not called up until

1940. In June 1941 he was posted to the Middle East where he joined the Notts Sherwood Rangers Yeomanry. Given a staff job at the base, he left to rejoin his regiment of his own accord and fought his way, as a tank officer in the North African Campaign, from Alamein to Tunisia. Whilst at Cairo he met G. S. Fraser, Lawrence Durrell and Bernard Spencer, and his work was published in *Personal Landscape*. In December 1943 he returned to London and in June 1944 he was killed in the opening of the Second Front in Normandy. His work is contained in the following volumes:

Selected Poems, with John Hall and Norman Nicholson (Bale & Staples, 1943).

Alamein to Zem Zem (Editions Poetry London, 1947) a prose account of his experiences in the North African Campaign.

Collected Poems, edited by G. S. Fraser and John Waller (Editions Poetry London, 1951).

Selected Poems, edited by Ted Hughes (Faber and Faber, 1964).

Sidney Keyes

Born at Dartford, Kent, in 1922 (d. 1943), his mother dying shortly after he was born. He was educated at Tonbridge, where he won a history scholarship to Queen's College, Oxford, going up in October 1940. He was commissioned in the Queen's Own Royal West Kent Regiment in September, 1942. Left England with his regiment for North Africa in March 1943 and was killed in the Tunisian Campaign after a fortnight's active service. His poetry is contained in the following volumes, all published by Routledge:

The Iron Laurel, 1942.

The Cruel Solstice, 1944.

Collected Poems of Sidney Keyes, 1945.

In 1948 a collection of his plays and stories, with selections from his notebooks, letters and some unpublished poems, *Minos of Crete*, was edited by Michael Meyer.

Henry Reed

Born at Birmingham in 1914, he was educated at Birmingham University where he took his M.A. Worked as a free-lance journalist for a time and contributed to the *Birmingham Post* and *Manchester Guardian*. Called up in 1941, he served with the R.A.O.C., but was released in 1942 and took up an appointment at the Foreign Office. His only publications during the forties were:'

A Map of Verona (Cape, 1946).
The Novel since 1939, criticism, 1946.

Roy Fuller

Born at Oldham, Lancs, in 1912. He served in the Fleet Air Arm of the Royal Navy from 1941 to 1946 and until recently worked in London as a solicitor to a large Building Society. Was elected Professor of Poetry at Oxford in 1968. He has written several novels, including *The Second Curtain*, *Fantasy and Fugue*, *Image of a Society*, *The Ruined Boys*, and *The Father's Comedy*, and stories for children (*Savage Gold*, *With My Little Eye*). His poetry written in the forties was published in the following volumes:
The Middle of a War (Hogarth, 1942).
A Lost Season (Hogarth, 1944).
Epitaphs and Occasions (Lehmann, 1949).

Edith Sitwell

Born at Scarborough, Yorks, in 1887, daughter of Sir George Sitwell, and sister of Sir Osbert and Sacheverell Sitwell. Educated privately. Made Dame Grand Cross of the Order of the British Empire, 1954. Joined the Roman Catholic Church in 1954. She edited many anthologies of poetry. Among her biographical and critical works are: *Alexander Pope* (1930), *The English Eccentrics* (1933), *Aspects of Modern Poetry* (1934), *Victoria of England* (1936) *A Poet's Notebook* (1943), *Fanfare for Elizabeth* (1946). Her poetry of the forties is included in the following volumes all published by Macmillan:
Street Songs, 1942.
Green Song, 1944.
The Song of the Cold, 1945.
The Canticle of the Rose, 1949.

Edwin Muir

Born at Deerness, a small island in the Orkneys, in 1887 and educated at Kirkwall Burgh School. When he was fourteen his family moved to Glasgow, where he started work as an office-boy and later became a clerk in commercial and shipbuilding companies. He married Willa Anderson in 1919 and moved to London, where he took up journalism. Travelled widely in Europe from 1921 onwards. Taught for the British Council 1942–50. In 1945 he was sent by the British Council to Prague, and in 1949 to Rome, as Director of the British Council Institute. Warden of Newbattle Abbey, near Edinburgh, 1950–55. Died at Addenbrookes Hospital, Cambridge, in 1959. Muir and his wife translated Kafka into English. Muir's prose work includes *The Marionettes*, a novel (1927), *The Structure of the Novel* (1928), *John Knox* (1929), *The Three Brothers* (1931), *Poor Tom* (1932), *Scottish Journey* (1935), *The Story and the Fable* (1940), *Essays in Literature and Society* (1949) and *The Estate of Poetry* (1962). His poetry of the forties was published in the following volumes all published by Faber:
The Narrow Place, 1943.
The Voyage, 1946.
The Labyrinth, 1949.

Vernon Watkins

Born in Maesteg, Wales, in 1906 (d. 1967). Educated at Repton and Magdalene College, Cambridge. Worked most of his life in Lloyds Bank, Swansea, interrupted by service in the R.A.F. from 1941 to 1946. His poetry of the forties is contained in the following volumes, all published by Faber:
The Ballad of the Mari Lwyd, 1941.
The Lamp and the Veil, 1945.
The Lady with the Unicorn, 1948.

Dylan Thomas

Born in Swansea, Wales, in 1914 (died in New York, 1953) and educated at the local grammar school. He was a reporter with the *South Wales Evening Post* for a time, and worked with the B.B.C.

during the war. His prose work consists of *Quite Early One Morning* (1954), broadcast talks, and *Portrait of the Artist as a Young Dog*, short stories, 1940; and his dramatic work *The Doctor and the Devils*, a screen play, 1953, and *Under Milk Wood* (1954), a play for voices, commissioned by the B.B.C. The only volume of poems published during the forties was *Deaths and Entrances* (Dent, 1946), but this is generally acknowledged to contain his finest work. His *Collected Poems 1934–52* (Dent, 1953) contained only six new poems.

Norman Nicholson

Born at Millom, Cumberland, in 1914, where he still lives. Educated at local schools. Lectured for a time for the Workers' Educational Association. Edited the *Penguin Anthology of Religious Verse*, 1942. Nicholson has written several verse dramas, including *The Old Man of the Mountains* (1946), *Prophesy to the Wind* (1952), and *Built by Drowning* (1960). His prose work includes *Man and Literature* (1943), criticism; *The Fire of the Lord* (1944), novel; and *William Cowper* (1960). His poetry of the forties, published by Faber, appears in the following volumes:
Five Rivers, 1944.
Rock Face, 1948.
He shared a volume with John Hall and Keith Douglas, *Selected Poems*, published by Bale and Staples in 1942.

Further Reading

Literary Criticism
BLACKBURN, T., *The Price of an Eye*, Longmans, 1961.
BRINNIN, J. M., *Dylan Thomas in America*, Dent, 1957.
BUTTER, P., *Edwin Muir, Man and Poet*, Oliver & Boyd, 1966.
ELIOT, T. S., *Notes Towards the Definition of Culture*, Faber, 1948.
FITZGIBBON, C., *The Life of Dylan Thomas*, Dent, 1965.
FRASER, G. S., *The Modern Writer and His World,* Penguin,
    1953, 1964; *Vision and Rhetoric*, Faber, 1959.
GRAVES, R., *The White Goddess*, Faber, 1959.
PRESS, J. *Rule and Energy*, Oxford University Press, 1963.
RAINE, K. *Defending Ancient Springs*, Oxford University Press,
    1967.
SPENDER, S., *Life and the Poet,* Secker & Warburg, 1942.

Political
ATTLEE, C. R., *As It Happened*, Heinemann, 1954.
BOOTHBY, R., *I Fight to Live*, Gollancz, 1947.
BEVERIDGE, LORD, *Power and Influence*, Hodder & Stoughton,
    1953.
BEVERIDGE, J., *Beveridge and His Plan*, Hodder & Stoughton,
    1954.
BULLOCK, A., *Ernest Bevin* (esp. Vol. 2) Heinemann, 1967.
CHURCHILL, W. S., *The Second World War*, 6 vols., Cassell,
    1948–54.
DALTON, H., *The Fateful Years*, Muller, 1957.
SHINWELL, E., *Conflict without Malice*, Odhams, 1955.
WOOLTON, LORD, *Memoirs*, Cassell, 1959.

Social History, War and Postwar Background
BRIGGS, A., *Friends of the People*, Batsford, 1956.
BUREAU OF CURRENT AFFAIRS, *The First Eighteen Months*,
    Penguin, 1947.
CALDER, A., *The People's War: Britain 1939–45*, Cape, 1969.
CHURCHILL, W. S., *The Sinews of Peace*, Cassell, 1948.
FLEMING, P., *Invasion 1940*, Hart-Davis, 1959.

FYFE, H., *Britain's Wartime Revolution*, Gollancz, 1944.

GREGG, P., *The Welfare State*, Harrap, 1967.

HILLARY, R., *The Last Enemy*, Macmillan, 1962.

HOPKINS, H., *The New Look*, Secker & Warburg, 1963.

MARSH, D., *The Changing Structure of England and Wales, 1871–1951*, Routledge, 1958.

MONTGOMERY, B. L., *Memoirs*, Collins, 1958.

MORAN, LORD, *Winston Churchill—The Struggle for Survival 1940–65*, Constable, 1966.

NICOLSON, H., *Diaries and Letters 1939–45*, Collins, 1967.

ORWELL, G., *The Lion and the Unicorn*, Secker & Warburg, 1941.

Collected Essays, Journalism and Letters, 4 vols., Secker & Warburg, 1968.

ROSS, A., *The Forties*, Weidenfeld & Nicolson, 1950.

SCOTT, J. D., *Life in Britain*, Eyre & Spottiswoode, 1956.

TAYLOR, A. J. P., *English History 1914–45*, Oxford University Press, 1965.

TITMUSS, R., *Essays on the Welfare State*, Allen & Unwin, 1958.

TURNER, E. S., *The Phoney War*, Joseph, 1961.

WATKINS, E., *The Cautious Revolution*, Secker & Warburg, 1951.